indigo knits

indigo knits

THE QUINTESSENTIAL GUIDE TO DENIM YARN FROM THE FOUNDERS OF ARTWORK

Jane Gottelier

Photography by
PATRICK GOTTELIER

POTTER
CRAFT

Copyright © 2007 by Patrick Gottelier and Jane Gottelier

All projects are original designs for the founders of *Artwork*®

All rights reserved.

Published in the United States by Potter Craft, an imprint
of the Crown Publishing Group, a division of Random
House, Inc., New York.
www.crownpublishing.com
www.pottercraft.com

POTTER CRAFT and CLARKSON N. POTTER are
trademarks, and POTTER and colophon are registered
trademarks of Random House, Inc.

Library of Congress Cataloging-in-Publication Data
Gottelier, Jane.
    Indigo knits : the quintessential guide to denim yarn
from the Founders of Artwork / Jane Gottelier;
photography by Patrick Gottelier. — 1st ed.
        p.   cm.
Includes index.
ISBN 978-0-307-35220-0
1. Knitting.   2. Yarn.   3. Indigo.   I. Title.
TT820.G78   2007
746.43'2—dc22   2007008462

Printed in China

Design by Susi Oberhelman

10 9 8 7 6 5 4 3 2 1

First Edition

contents

Introduction

Prussia Cove in the spring.

When we first began the Artwork fashion label in 1977, we had no studio and no employees. Nevertheless, Whistles, a boutique in Central London (now a successful chain), had placed an order with us for twenty-four pieces of hand-knitwear, and we were determined to fill it. So we enlisted Patrick's mother, Freda, who organized a modest fifteen knitters, all from the town of Penzance, to finish the garments. We carried out the design, packing, and administrative duties from our small basement apartment in North London. Deliveries were made in our red Mini.

We had no idea those initial pieces were going to be such a success, but they were, and we received a reorder from Whistles within days. Freda wisely increased our number of knitters, which was just in time, because Lucille Lewin, the owner of Whistles, phoned up again to tell us she had a buyer from Macy's in her store who wanted to place a large order with us. Suddenly we had a hand-knitting business and an international one to boot! Before long, we had our first trade show in New York, and we were in full fashion cycle, producing themed collections two to four times a year and traveling the world selling our designs. Meanwhile, by the early 1990s we had more than a thousand hand knitters working for us throughout England, the largest such group in the UK.

So, from day one Artwork has been an eclectic mix of fashion, knitting, and Cornwall. Through insane dinners in Milan, press openings in Tokyo, trade shows in New York, and interviews in Paris, wherever we have been, whatever the trend, Cornwall has kept us grounded and provided us with some much-needed rest and relaxation. And the one yarn that has run through our designs like a connecting thread has been indigo-dyed cotton. It has fascinated and fed us! The versatility of cotton and the ever-changing hues of indigo: These qualities have allowed us to design garments that are slick, sexy, and city one season and robust, rough, and rustic the next.

The old harbor in Newlyn.

In *Indigo Knits*, we hope to share some of the trade secrets we've developed during our twenty-five years of developing innovative knitwear designs. Before you begin the projects in the book, please read through the section on "Working with Indigo Yarn." Here, we cover some of the basics of indigo-dyed yarn, with special emphasis on how to wash and distress your indigo knitwear. We'll also highlight some of the exciting possibilities for applying different treatments and finishes to your indigo knitwear. The projects themselves do not require knitting expertise—there's something here for everyone, from classic cables, stripes, and intarsia to crochet, beading, and just plain knitting.

Of course we couldn't devote an entire book to indigo knitwear without also sharing our love of Cornwall. To that end, we've attempted to capture the colors and moods of particular Cornish locales through our choice of projects. And all of Patrick's photography is set on location in the picturesque villages and beautiful seascapes of Cornwall. We've also provided a bit of historical background and insider travel tips on Cornwall—just in case you decide to pack up your knitting needles for a visit to the place that has inspired so much of our work.

Enjoy!

JANE AND PATRICK GOTTELIER
www.artworkbygottelier.co.uk

Working with Indigo Yarn

Loading the lobster pots, Newlyn.

I FIRST CAME ACROSS INDIGO YARN IN THE 1980s while doing research into new yarns and fabrics for a summer collection at the Cotton Institute in London. I knew I was onto something huge the moment I saw a few balls of Michael Quinnen's machine-knit yarn. Michael, an engineering graduate, began his career as a fashion designer for the jeans label Stirling Cooper back in the 1970s. He was working on a design for a woven denim jacket, but he couldn't find a denim yarn that would work for the cuffs and trims. While indigo-dyed yarn did exist, it was unsuitable for knitting. That's when Michael hit upon the idea for a machine-knit indigo-dyed yarn and began to develop a process to create it. He worked on the problem until by 1984 he had not only devised a new dyeing method—rope dyeing and splitting the yarn into cones—he had patented his system in the UK and the United States as well.

Patrick and I agreed that a handknit version of Michael's yarn was an ingenious idea, so we called him up to ask for his help. Together, the three of us translated Michael's machine-knit yarn to a handknit weight, working out the shrinkage and the fading qualities and testing our results by knitting a few sample garments.

The first time we used the new indigo yarn, in an early Artwork collection, it went fairly unnoticed. We then decided to take an entirely different route, creating a men's fashion label we called George Trowark (an anagram of Artwork). Traditional with a twist, our first piece was a Cornish fisherman's sweater knitted in indigo cotton instead of the traditional wool (a similar version appears on page 28). The label became a great success, and although it was aimed at men, an awful lot of women were buying the sweaters, too! The next stage was to give women an indigo-knits label of their own—and that's how Artwork was born.

A Brief History of Indigo

The indigo plant is a small shrub that can grow to a height of anywhere between two and six feet (61–183cm). It has a single, woody stem, deep-green oval leaves (from which the dye is obtained), and delicate clusters of red flowers that resemble butterflies. The two main species of indigo plant are *Indigofera tinctoria* (native to Asia and India) and *Indigo suffructicosa* (native to Central and South America), but there are over three hundred known varieties of the plant.

Because indigo was discovered at different times and in different civilizations throughout the world, its dyeing methods and its uses vary considerably. Indigo-dyed fabrics have been found in Egyptian tombs dating back to the second century BC and in cloth produced in China as far back as the Han Dynasty. In Europe, indigo was not used as a dye until new trade routes opened up in Asia, India, and South America during the sixteenth century. The demand for indigo grew rapidly, and by the end of the sixteenth century Europeans set up their own plantations in tropical climates around the world, notably in Jamaica and South Carolina. By the end of the nineteenth century, indigo dye was commonly used for making uniforms as well as woolen fisherman's sweaters, and synthetic indigo had almost completely superseded the natural dye. Today, nearly all indigo dye is synthetic—its largest use is, of course, for blue jeans.

Characteristics of Indigo Yarn

As a dye, indigo is unpredictable. The indigo on freshly dyed cotton has a tendency to rub off on anything it comes into contact with, and no two batches are quite alike—plus it fades! At first, you may find these facts about indigo-dyed yarn rather daunting, but armed with some basic knowledge and techniques, you can make the qualities of this mercurial yarn work to your advantage. In fact, caring for your indigo knits is actually quite simple. Gone are the days of gentle hand-washing, lying flat, and easing back into shape. All denim knits actually achieve their original shape when you machine wash and tumble dry! What's more, they look better and better with every washing.

Here are a few other characteristics of indigo-dyed yarn to consider as you begin the projects in the book.

STAPLE

Staple is a term that refers to the length of an individual fiber. The longer the cotton staple, the smoother, more fluid, and longer lasting the yarn. Conversely, the shorter the staple, the more rustic the look (think old-fashioned dishcloth cotton). Staple is really a question of personal taste, but you might find a long-staple yarn more suitable for a project like the Lady Dona Ruffle Top (page 88), while the Cornish Knit Frock (page 24) might benefit from a rougher yarn.

RING SPUN VERSUS OPEN SPUN

At Artwork, the yarn we work with for indigo dyeing is usually open-spun cotton, as we think the finished result has a little more character. Ring-spun yarn provides a smoother finish and is perhaps better suited for projects that require a more fluid drape.

ROPE DYED VERSUS VAT DYED

Rope dyeing separates each "end" of the yarn, dyeing it primarily on the surface (badly, some might say), leaving the core of the yarn white, or natural. As the surface dye is washed or worn off the finished project, you will notice brighter contrasts in the fabric. Just look at the seams of your favorite old pair of jeans and you will see what I mean. Vat dyeing, on the other hand, is a more efficient method. The yarn is placed inside a pressurized vat, which tends to disperse the dye more evenly. More consistent and better for quality control, vat-dyed yarn lacks that extra bit of character. The difference between rope-dyed and vat-dyed yarn will become more visible with wear and washing.

GLORIOUS INCONSISTENCY

The most important issue to consider when working with indigo yarn is the wonderfully inconsistent nature of the indigo dye itself. Patrick and I once had a meeting with a very senior chemist at a large fiber company to discuss the ways in which we could help him supply indigo dye to a retailer concerned with "quality control." At one point, the chemist leaned back in his chair and sighed. "You know," he said, "if indigo were invented as a dye today, it would probably be rejected out of hand because it is so *!@# difficult to standardize." That's exactly why Patrick and I love it!

The other issue to keep in mind—and this applies to

all denim yarn—is shrinkage. As you begin the projects in this book, you may notice that many of the garments look a bit larger than you might expect. Do not worry! That's because the patterns are designed 20 percent longer than is customary in order to compensate for the shrinkage that will occur when you first wash your finished piece. If you're new to denim yarn, you might want to begin with one of the accessories, just to learn about shrinkage on a project where size is not so critical.

FADING AND COLOR

Indigo-dyed yarn typically comes in three basic shades of blue—dark, mid, and pale—all of which are going to wash out and fade naturally over time. The more you wash your indigo knit, the more it will fade. As I mentioned previously, the indigo dye will rub off until you've washed your finished garment. Your hands will pick up the indigo dye while you're knitting. But don't be alarmed—soap and water soon gets it off.

The fourth available shade of denim yarn, ecru (a natural cream color), does not fade. Ecru is not actually indigo-dyed, but the yarn consists of the same cotton used for indigo dyeing and, thus, you will need to follow the washing and drying instructions on pages 10–11. It's wonderful as a counterpoint to the various indigo shades, and I couldn't resist including a few projects knit in ecru.

When choosing a denim yarn, always consider the shade carefully. At Artwork, we tend to prefer the darkest indigos available, since you can always make a dark shade paler but you can't make a pale shade darker. To see the difference between the three shades of blue, turn to the Painterly Stripe Sweater (page 17), which calls for all four colors of denim yarn.

Distressing Techniques

Fading occurs naturally with indigo-dyed denim yarn, just as it does with your favorite pair of jeans. You can help this process along with a few simple techniques. Keep in mind as you are distressing your knitted pieces that textural stitches, such as cables and seed stitches, distress better. This is because protruding stitches like these are more likely to wear down in the washing and drying processes. Fringe also distresses fabulously. After you take a fringed garment out of the washing machine, you will notice that the cut ends of the fringe have unraveled and the ends have turned paler, giving your garment an amazing vintage feel.

Caring for Denim Knits

WASHING

Washing is an essential part of caring for all denim knits. Not only does it restore the original shape of your garment, it improves its appearance! Before you wash your garment, always make sure that it is fully sewn up and that you have stitched it together firmly with the same yarn that you knitted it with. Then follow these three simple steps.

Step 1. Place your finished item in the washing machine, thowing in some denim jeans or any other denim fabrics you might own (unless this is a project knit in ecru

Tools you'll need to distress your indigo knitwear:

- Large plastic container
- Several smaller plastic containers
- Apron
- Rubber gloves
- Pegs
- Household paint brushes
- Sandpaper
- Bleach
- Large plastic sheet or protective covering for work surface
- Drying rack
- Household string
- Sponge
- Saucer

yarn). These garments help generate some additional friction, which, in turn, creates a more distressed look.

Step 2. Then run the machine on the WARM cycle (104 degrees Fahrenheit [40 degrees Celsius]). Be sure to include some fabric softener to prevent the cotton from getting stiff and some inexpensive powder detergent to help with the distressing.

Note: Water temperatures will vary among washing machines according to the temperature at which you're water heater is set. If you're unsure as to whether the WARM setting on your machine corresponds to 104 degrees Fahrenheit (40 degrees Celsius), you may want to test the water temperature using a thermometer. Then, if necessary, adjust your water heater setting accordingly. Alternatively, try calculating shrinkage by knitting a gauge swatch and washing it on WARM. If the swatch has shrunk more than the 20 percent alotted for in the patterns (refer to the Yarn Substitution information on page 157 for instructions on how to calculate shrinkage), then you'll want to use a lower water temperature.

Step 3. When the cycle is finished, take out the garments and run the machine again to prevent future washes from picking up any residual dye.

DRYING

Now that you have washed your garment, you are ready to shrink it to the appropriate size by placing it in the dryer. The dryer also creates even more friction with which to wear down the dye.

Step 1. Place your knit in the dryer and dry on HOT for approximately one hour. For small garments, you may need less drying time.

Step 2. Remove the knit from the dryer before it is completely dry.

If you do not have a dryer at home, lay the knit flat on a towel in a warm room, or leave it outside in the sun to let it dry naturally. Never drape denim knits over a radiator, as this will make them stretch.

IRONING AND STEAMING

When you take your garment out of the dryer, it will need to be steamed back into shape. A steam iron is the best tool for this task. If you do not have a steam iron, you can use an ordinary dry iron and a damp cloth, and iron through the cloth. You can be quite rough with your denim knits, as the cotton is practically indestructible!

RUBBING

For an even more distressed look, try using a damp pumice stone or sandpaper to rub some of the indigo off the textured stitches.

Rubbing with sandpaper

All-Over Bleaching Method

For those knitters who are too impatient to wait for their sweaters to age naturally, bleaching offers a quick fix. As with most shortcuts, this one is not quite as effective as the real thing (fading over time), but the results are still quite good.

If you are going to use any of the bleaching techniques in this book, we recommend that you knit a swatch first, because if the bleaching goes awry, there is no way of correcting it. In order to repeat the process accurately, record the exact method you used to bleach your swatch, right down to the brand of bleach. I have found that different brands of bleach vary dramatically in strength and effectiveness, so do be sure to experiment whenever you try a new kind.

Also, when working with bleach, always remember to protect your hands by wearing rubber gloves! If possible, work outside or in a well-ventilated room.

To achieve an all-over lightening (or bleaching) on your knitting, you can use either the washing-machine method or the hand method.

WASHING-MACHINE METHOD

This method will help you achieve immediate results, but

you will have less control over the end product.

Step 1. Soak the knitted item in a sink of cold water until it is thoroughly wet.

Step 2. Place the knitted item in the washing machine and run the machine on the WARM cycle (104 degrees Fahrenheit [40 degrees Celsius]). Meanwhile, dissolve 6¾ tablespoons (100ml) of household bleach in an equal amount of cold water. Add the bleach via the soap dispenser after the machine has run for fifteen minutes. Allow the wash cycle to finish.

Step 3: Check to see if your garment is the desired shade of indigo. If so, then add some inexpensive powder detergent and fabric softener, and wash the item again on WARM (104 degrees Fahrenheit [40 degrees Celsius]) to ensure that all the bleach is washed out. To lighten your garment even more, add more bleach and wash again.

HAND METHOD

Although this method is longer and more involved, it does give you more control over the bleaching process.

Step 1. Fill a bathtub, sink, or bowl with cold water, and allow the knitted item to soak until it is thoroughly wet. Remove the item and ring out the water.

Step 2. Refill the tub, sink, or bowl you just used with 4¼ cups (1 liter) of cold water. Then add 6¾ tablespoons (100ml) of household bleach. Using a wooden spoon, swish the bleach around. The bleach should be fully dissolved in the water.

Step 3. Place the wet knit back in the tub, sink, or bowl, submerging it and swishing it gently in the water. Be very careful not to get water in your eyes!

Step 4. This is important. Do not leave the room, as bleach can take very quickly. As soon as the knit has achieved the hue you want, take it out and place it in a plastic bowl while you drain the water from the bleach-filled container. If the piece takes a while to bleach, you might need to add more bleach solution.

Step 5. You now have a choice: You can either wash out the bleach in the washing machine or wash out the bleach by hand. I suggest the machine, as it is more thorough. If you do opt for the machine, be sure to select the WARM cycle (104 degrees Fahrenheit [40 degrees Celsius]).

Step 6. Place the knitted item in the dryer or hand-dry it flat on a towel.

Note: Garments that have been bleached will retain more indigo dye around the seams, where it is more difficult for the bleach to penetrate. This is exactly how blue jeans behave when bleached.

Other Bleaching Techniques

Other bleaching techniques we've developed over the years include painting with bleach, dip bleaching, sponging, and tie-dye bleaching. These techniques work just as well on a simple garter stitch sweater as they do on a more complicated cable garment. If you're nervous about bleaching your newly knitted creation, then try experimenting with an old pair of jeans. It's not quite the same as bleaching a handknit, but you'll get the idea.

PAINTING WITH BLEACH

Indigo knitwear lends itself beautifully as a canvas on which to paint with bleach. **Always be sure to wear rubber gloves and an apron or overalls when painting with bleach.** I also suggest that you work outside if possible.

Step 1. Spread a clean towel or sheet on the ground.

Step 2. Lay the knitted item you want to bleach flat on the towel or fabric. If you want the bleach effects on the back of the knit to look different from those on the front, then place some plastic shopping bags inside the item to stop the bleach from leaking through.

Step 3. Dip any size brush in a bowl of bleach and begin painting your design of choice (a few design ideas are featured on pages 13–14). The bleach will usually take effect fairly quickly, but wait until you have achieved the desired contrast before you move on to step 4.

Step 4. As soon as you have created a design you like at the desired contrast, wash the item. You can either place the bleached item in the washing machine or wash out the bleach by hand. If you do opt for the machine, be sure to select the WARM cycle (104 degrees Fahrenheit [40 degrees Celsius]).

Step 5. Dry the item flat on a towel or place it in the dryer and run the machine on HOT for approximately one hour before checking on it. Remove the garment before it is completely dry.

BLEACH DESIGN IDEAS

Geometric

Stripes, diamonds, and squares always look nice. You can even use a metal ruler if you want your shapes to be precise, or let the lines wiggle for a free-form look.

Geometric

Abstract

Using several different thicknesses of paintbrushes, just draw whatever comes into your head. If you need more inspiration, use a picture from an art book or a postcard from an art gallery as a reference.

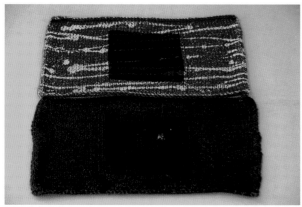

Abstract

Jackson Pollock

This technique is fascinating and easy. It can also get quite messy, so cover yourself up well! Once you have laid the knit flat on a towel, saturate your brush with bleach. Using flicking movements, splash the bleach all over the knitting. You should get some lovely random squiggles and lines. It's a real exercise in freedom of expression.

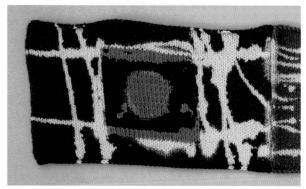

Jackson Pollock

Trompe l'Oeil

This is an effect we have used at Artwork quite a lot over the years. In the example below, we have painted a trompe l'oeil cable on the panel of a quilted beach blanket, but you can use any sort of figurative imagery you want.

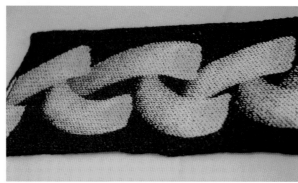

Trompe l'Oeil

Tracing with Bleach

If your knit includes cables or geometric lace patterns, you can trace around the stitches with bleach. The outline created by a small paintbrush will give the stitches new and interesting depths.

Tracing with Bleach

Bleaching on Intarsia

This technique can look very dramatic, particularly if you are knitting in intarsia using three different shades of indigo (below).

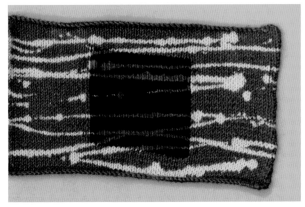

Bleaching on Intarsia

Bleaching on Stripes

The Painterly Stripe Sweater (page 106) uses this technique. To create the circular design, we traced around a bowl using a paintbrush. For a two-color stripe, we have an even easier suggestion. Purchase bleach that comes in a soft, squeezable container with a narrow spout. Then simply squeeze the bleach directly from the container onto the knitting to achieve an instant four-color stripe.

Bleaching on Stripes

Sponging

The effects that you can get with sponging are generally softer and less dense than those created by painting with brushes. To sponge your garment, simply dip a sponge into a saucer of bleach, squeeze out the excess bleach, and dab the sponge onto the knitting.

Sponging

STENCIL PRINTING WITH BLEACH

You might also consider using the simple stencil templates available at craft and hobby stores to embellish your denim knits. Simply dip the template into a saucer of bleach, allowing any excess bleach to drip off, and press the stencil against the knitted fabric. Here we have used a rose design.

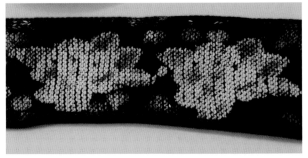

Stencil Printing with Bleach

DIP BLEACHING

This is a very simple technique that can only be done by hand. The result is a stunning fade. **Please be sure to wear rubber gloves and an apron or overalls.**

Step 1. Create a bleach mixture in a bowl, bath, or sink. You can either use a 50/50 mixture of bleach and cold water, or you can use 100 percent bleach. We prefer using 100 percent bleach, but keep in mind that you will have to act very quickly once the bleach starts to react on the knitting.

Step 2. Pin the item onto a drying rack or chair, and position the rack or chair next to the bleach mixture you just prepared. Lower the bottom of the garment, as much as you'd like bleached, into the mixture.

Dip Bleaching

Step 3. Watch carefully as the bleach mixture travels up the knit. You will notice that the bottom of the piece takes the bleach first. The upper part will also be affected but not as intensely. Eventually, a lovely blurred stripe will begin to appear. As soon as you have achieved the desired effect, take the knitting out of the bleach and machine-wash it on WARM (104 degrees Fahrenheit [40 degrees Celsius]) with detergent.

Step 4. Dry the knit flat on a towel, or place it in the dryer on HOT for approximately one hour before checking on it. Remove the garment before it is completely dry.

DIP BLEACHING FRINGE

Dip bleaching fringe creates a wonderful fade effect, as illustrated by the Fringe Bardot Top (page 52). You can bleach the fringe either before or after you attach it to the garment. Ideally, you should choose fringe that has cut ends, rather than looped ends, as they soak up the bleach better. Refer to the instructions for dip bleaching (above),

and note that you only need to immerse the ends of the fringe in the bleach mixture.

Dip Bleaching Fringe

TIE-DYE BLEACHING

This technique lends indigo knits a very summery, '60s look. **Just be sure to wear rubber gloves and an apron or overalls.**

Step 1. Using regular household string, tie up your item very tightly at various, random points. Remember: Where the string is tightly tied, the indigo color will not be bleached out. If you want a lot of the indigo color to remain, you will need to bind the piece of knitting many times over so that it can successfully resist the bleach.

Step 2. Make up a bleach mixture in a bowl, bath, or sink. You can use either a 50/50 mixture of bleach and cold water or 100 percent bleach. Next, submerge the bundle in the mixture, watching carefully to see changes in color developing. As soon as you have achieved the desired color on the visible portions of the knit, take the bundle out of the bleach mixture and lay it on a towel to dry.

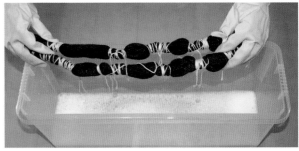

Tie-Dye Bleaching

Step 3. Remove the string that binds the knitting, using scissors if necessary. Shake the item back into shape, and immediately submerge the item in a bowl, sink, or bath of cold water. You should see an amazing tie-dye bleach pattern on your garment. Remove the item from the rinse and squeeze it to remove all the excess bleach. Then, place the item in a third bowl and put it in the washing machine right away. Wash it on WARM (104 degrees Fahrenheit [40 degrees Celsius]) with detergent and fabric softener.

Step 4. Dry the item flat on a towel or place it in the dryer on HOT for approximately one hour before checking on it. Remove the garment before it is bone dry.

Step 5. Steam the garment back into shape using a steam iron.

Decorating Indigo Knitwear

These are just a few of the ways you can embellish your indigo-dyed knitwear.

EMBROIDERY

Garments or homewares knit in indigo cotton can be embroidered just like any other knitting, as shown in the Gwithian Beach Blanket (page 58). The only difference is that the indigo yarn will bleed into the embroidery when washed if you are using cotton-based or most other natural threads. Cotton-polyester blends will only partially absorb the dye, while most synthetic fibers will resist the dye entirely. If you are using a cotton thread and you wish to disguise the bleed, then embroider onto the knitted denim in woven denim and blue embroidery threads. Always be sure to choose threads that can withstand a hot wash.

OVERSTITCHING

This is an easy and extremely effective way to enhance a piece of denim knitting, with dramatic results. Overstitching can be used to emphasize a real or a fake seam, as shown in the Sailmaker Bolero (page 142).

PATCHING

Patching can be used on any portion of a knitted garment in order to prolong its wear. It can also be done for purely aesthetic reasons. When selecting patches for a piece of indigo knitting, it is always better to choose a woven denim (preferably cut from a pair of old jeans) that is similar in weight and wear to the piece of knitting you will be attaching it to. If you are starting off with new indigo yarn, then attach new denim so they can be worn down together.

SWISS DARNING

This technique involves tracing over stitches with embroidery, to exaggerate or decorate your knitting. We have used this it on the back of the Artist's Waistcoat (page 70) to make the knitted fabric look like a woven, pinstriped, Victorian gentleman's waistcoat.

WEAVE-STITCHING

If you like to sew, then weave-stitching is a great way to add interest and depth to your knitting. It can be quite time consuming, but the final result is well worth it. All you do is thread a running stitch through the knitting at various, random places, using any indigo yarn threaded onto a fat needle. The Sequined Throw (page 124) and the Gwithian Beach Bag (page 56) both call for this technique.

Weave-Stitching

Abbreviations and Techniques

Knitting

alt: Alternate, alternating.

beg: Begin, beginning.

BC: Slip next stitch onto cable needle and hold at back, knit stitch through back of loop (to twist stitch), then p1 from cable needle.

BC2: Slip next stitch onto cable needle and hold at back, k2, then k1 from cable needle.

C3B: Slip next stitch onto cable needle and leave at back, k2, then k1 from cable needle.

C3F: Slip next 2 stitches onto cable needle and hold at front, k1, then k2 from cable needle.

C4B: Slip next 2 stitches onto cable needle and hold at back, k2 from left-hand needle, then k2 from cable needle.

C4F: Slip next 2 stitches onto cable needle and hold at front, k2 from left-hand needle, then k2 from cable needle.

C6B: Slip next 3 stitches onto cable needle and hold at back, k3 from left-hand needle, then k3 from cable needle.

C6F: Slip next 3 stitches onto cable needle and hold at front, k3 from left-hand needle, then k3 from cable needle.

C8B: Slip next 4 stitches onto cable needle and leave at back, k4 from left-hand needle, then k4 from cable needle.

cont: Continue, continuing.

CR5: Slip next 3 stitches onto cable needle and leave at front, k2, place last stitch onto cable needle, back onto left-hand needle, purl this stitch, then k2 from cable needle.

CR14: Slip next 4 stitches onto cable needle and hold at front, slip next 6 stitches onto 2nd cable needle and leave at back, k4 from left-hand needle, then k6 from cable needle at back, then k4 from cable needle at front.

CR5B: Slip next stitch onto cable needle and hold at back, k4 from left-hand needle, then p1 from cable needle.

CR5F: Slip next 4 stitches onto cable needle and hold at front, p1 from left-hand needle, then k4 from cable needle.

CR7L: Slip next 3 stitches onto cable needle and hold at front, [knit through back of loop, p1] twice, then [knit through back of loop, p1, knit through back of loop] from cable needle.

CR7R: Slip next 4 stitches onto cable needle and hold at back, knit through back of loop, p1, knit through back of loop over next 3 stitches, then [p1, knit through back of loop] twice from cable needle.

dec: Decrease.

FC: Slip next stitch onto cable needle and hold at front, p1, then knit through back of loop from cable needle.

FC2: Slip next 2 stitches onto cable needle and leave at front, k1, then k2 from cable needle.

foll: Following, follows.

garter st: Knit every row.

I-cord: Cast on required number of stitches with double-pointed needles. *Without turning work, slide stitches to right-hand end of needle, pull yarn around back of stitches and knit as usual. Repeat from * until cord is required length.

I-cord border: With circular needle, pick up appropriate number of stitches from edge to be bordered. Pull needle through so that you are ready to work from beginning of picked-up stitches (right side of work facing). Work I-cord edging as follows:

On separate needle, cast on 2 stitches. Transfer them to the circular needle holding the edge stitches. Now work as follows: *k1, slip 1, yo, k1 (from edge stitches), pass 2 slip stitches (the slipped stitch and the yo) over. Replace the 2 stitches on the right-hand needle to the left-hand needle and repeat from * to end of stitches. The border can be eased around corners (on collars, blankets, etc.) by working the 1st 2 stitches only once or twice before then carrying on from *.

inc: Increase.

k: Knit.

K1B: Knit stitch through back of loop (to twist the stitch).

K3B: K3 stitches through back of loop.

K1TBL: K1 stitch through back of loop.

k2tog: Knit next 2 stitches together.

kfb: Knit into front and back of next stitch.

k-wise: Knit-wise.

LT: Skip 1st stitch, knit into the back of 2nd stitch on left-hand needle, then insert right-hand needle through both the back of the skipped stitch and the 2nd stitch and knit both stitches together.

m1: Make 1. Pick up strand that lies between stitch just worked and next stitch, knit (or purl) into the back of it.

m1pw: Make 1 purl-wise.

p: Purl.

patt: Pattern.

P1B: Purl stitch through back of loop (to twist the stitch).

P3B: P3 stitches through back of loop.

pfb: Purl into front and back of next stitch.

psso: Pass a slipstitch over a knitted stitch.

p-wise: Purlwise.

rep: Repeat.

rev: Reverse.

rev st st: Reverse stockinette stitch (purl side is right side).

RS: Right side.

RT: Knit 2 together, leaving garter stitches on needle, then insert right-hand needle from front between the stitches and knit the 1st stitch again, then slip both stitches off the needle together.

skpo: Slip 1, k1, pass the slipped stitch over.

Sl 1 p-wise: Slip next stitch as if to purl.

ssk: Slip, slip, knit. Slip the next 2 stitches knit-wise, place tip of left-hand needle into front of these 2 stitches, and knit together.

st(s): Stitch(es).

st st: Stockinette stitch.

T2B: Slip next stitch onto cable needle and leave at back, knit through the back loop, then p1 from cable needle.

T2F: Slip next stitch onto cable needle and leave at front, p1, then knit through back of loop from cable needle.

T3B: Slip next stitch onto cable needle and leave at back, k2, then p1 from cable needle.

T3F: Slip next 2 stitches onto cable needle and leave at front, p1, then k2 from cable needle.

T4B: Slip next 2 stitches onto cable needle and hold at back, k2 from left-hand needle, purl stitches from cable needle.

T4F: Slip next 2 stitches onto cable needle and hold at front, p2 from left-hand needle, then knit stitches from cable needle.

tbl: Through the back loop.

WS: Wrong side.

w&t: Wrap and turn. If on a knit row, bring yarn to front of work, slip next stitch, take yarn to back of work, slip wrapped stitch back to left-hand needle. Turn work. If on a purl row, take yarn to back of work, slip next stitch, bring yarn to front of work, slip wrapped stitch back to left-hand needle, turn work.

y2rn: Yarn twice around needle.

yb: Yarn back. Take yarn to back of work.

yf: Yarn forward. Bring yarn to front of work.

yo: Yarn over. Bring yarn from back of work, over needle to the front and to the back again.

yp2: Yarn forward. Yarn around needle, p2, pass made stitch over 2 purled stitches.

Crochet

ch: Chain.

dc: Double crochet.

dc2tog: Double crochet 2 together

hdc: Half double crochet.

lp: Loop.

open tr: *Yo hook twice, insert hook into stitch, yo and draw loop through, [yo and draw through 2 loops on hook] twice*; rep from * to * for each open double triple crochet, leaving additional loop on hook each time.

sc: Single crochet.

sp: Space.

ss: Slip stitch.

tr: Triple crochet.

newlyn blue

Nestled between the picturesque harbor of Mousehole (pronounced MOU-zhill) and the Georgian town of Penzance lies Newlyn, a fishing village in the southwest corner of Cornwall. Its winding streets and alleyways are peppered higgledy-piggledy with fishermen's cottages leading down to the harbor. The name *Newlyn* derives from the Cornish word *lulyn*, meaning "fleet pool," a reference to the deep-water anchorage that once lay between Newlyn and Mousehole.

Historically, Newlyn is famous for two things—its fishing industry and its artists. The two are so inextricably linked that you cannot mention one without mentioning the other. Pilchard, or sardine, fishing was the main industry in Newlyn in the nineteenth century. Before 1870, boats used *seines* (large, weighted nets) to catch pilchards. In 1870, mackerel fishing, which utilized drift-boats and drivers, replaced seine-net fishing. This method allowed fishermen to venture much farther out to sea.

In the nineteenth century, fishing was a hard life for the whole family; when the fish did not come in, it affected everyone and brought many families to the brink of starvation. During this period, the church still expected destitute families to pay their tithes, and this could prove to be a particular burden for many hardworking people. One particular fishwife, an octogenarian by the name of Mary Kelynach, became famous for walking three hundred miles (483km) to London to protest her situation. Her feistiness became legendary among Britons, and she was even presented to Queen Victoria.

Today Newlyn employs one of the largest fishing fleets in England, exporting fish all over Europe. But even now, fishing can be a hard life and is not without its tragedies. On December 19, 1981, the *Solomon Browne*, the Newlyn lifeboat, went out to rescue the *Union Star*, a coaster adrift in an atrocious force-12 hurricane. Both boats were lost, and there wasn't a single family in this close-knit community that remained untouched by the tragedy. The village of Newlyn was a very sad place on Christmas day 1981. Every year since then, the festive Christmas lights of Newlyn and Mousehole have been turned off on December 19 in memory of those who lost their lives that day.

Thanks to the efforts of the artists affiliated with the Newlyn School of painters, the life of the nineteenth century Newlyn fisherman has been faithfully documented. Founded by the artist Stanhope Forbes and his wife, Elizabeth, the Newlyn School emerged from the Parisian Plein Air Movement. *Plein air* simply means "out of doors,"

> ## ➤ ART
>
> **Badcocks Gallery:** Great selection of contemporary art, with exhibitions that change monthly. www.badcocksgallery.co.uk
>
> **The Board School:** Fascinating collection of fishing paraphernalia. Contact Cornish Tourist Board for more information: www.cornwalltouristboard.co.uk.
>
> **Newlyn Art Gallery:** Exhibitions of contemporary art. Built by John Passmore Edwards, a Cornish philanthropist. www.newlynartgallery.co.uk
>
> **Penlee House Gallery and Museum:** Houses works by the Newlyn School of painters. Located in Penzance. www.penleehouse.org.uk

> ## ➤ REFRESHMENTS
>
> **Fish and chip shops:** Jewells (from classic cod and chips to some more unusual offerings), John Dory and Chips, Ray and Chips, Monk and Chips, and Lemon Sole and Chips.
>
> **Retail shops offering local fish:** Trelawneys Fish Store, W. Stevenson and Sons, W. Harveys and Sons (for excellent crab), and J. H. Turner and Co.
>
> **Jelberts Ice Cream Shop:** Just one flavor (vanilla) of this legendary ice cream. It has the taste and texture of sorbet, served in a cone with a generous blob of clotted cream and aerated chocolate bar on top.
>
> **Smugglers Restaurant:** Great food and seating that overlooks the harbor. Be sure to check out the painted sign. www.smugglersnewlyn.co.uk

Detail from *Tucking a School of Pilchards*, 1897, by Perry Robert Craft. Oil on canvas, Penlee House Gallery and Museum, Penzance.

Another view of Newlyn Harbor, an inspiration to the Newlyn School of artists.

or painting in the open air. The Plein Air Movement directed artists to record exactly what they saw, which, for the Newlyn artists, meant depicting the harsh working conditions of the local fishermen. The artists who settled in and around Newlyn formed a colony in the upper part of the village, an area known by locals, for some unknown reason, as California. Forbes and his wife started an art school there, which would soon become a mecca for artists in the nineteenth century. While the fishing folk who posed for these artists were at first puzzled when instructed to wear their everyday working clothes instead of their "Sunday best," the Newlyn painters have given us a glimpse into the life of these fishermen and fishwives that otherwise might have been lost to history.

The traditional clothing worn by fishing families along the coast inspired the projects in this chapter. Originally, conventional Guernseys and Cornish frocks were knit with a very tight, twisted, woolen yarn on small needles, giving these garments a tight appearance, as well as an invaluable waterproof quality. The needles were quite long and fine (in some cases 16" [112mm]), made of steel, and pointed at both ends. Modern knitters would probably prefer circular needles for this kind of work. The deep-blue, indigo-dyed, worsted yarn of the early Guernseys and knit frocks gradually faded through wear and tear, much as our cotton indigo yarn does when exposed to the elements. The colors ranged from gorgeous tones of soft cornflower-blue or sometimes, depending on what they were exposed to, soft hues of purple, green, or gray.

cornish knit frock

This sweater is probably the most traditional of them all, not to mention one of our first Artwork designs. You'll find examples of it in the paintings of fishermen by the Newlyn School artists, like the one shown on page 22, and in photographs from the early nineteenth century.

Sizes
S (M, L, XL)

Measurements after Washing
Chest: 37¾" (41¾", 45¾", 49¾") [96 (106, 116, 126)cm]
Length to shoulder: 25½", (26½", 27¼", 28") [65 (67, 69, 71)cm]
Sleeve length: 19" (19¼", 19¾", 20") [48 (49, 50, 51)cm]

Materials
▶ 18 (19, 21, 22) balls Elann Den-M-Nit (100% cotton, 1¾ oz [50g], 101 yd [92m]) in Pale Indigo
▶ Size 3 (3mm) needles
▶ Size 6 (4mm) needles
▶ Cable needle
▶ Sewing needle and thread

Gauge
20 sts and 28 rows = 4" (10cm) in st st using size 6 (4mm) needles before washing.

Abbreviations and Techniques
Refer to pages 18–19.

PANEL A
(worked over 14 sts)
Row 1 (RS): K2, p1, k11.
Row 2: P10, k1, p3.
Row 3: K4, p1, k9.
Row 4: P8, k1, p5.
Row 5: K6, p1, k7.
Row 6: P6, k1, p7.
Row 7: K8, p1, k5.
Row 8: P4, k1, p9.
Row 9: K10, p1, k3.
Row 10: P2, k1, p11.
Row 11: K12, p1, k1.
Row 12: As Row 10.
Row 13: As Row 9.
Row 14: As Row 8.
Row 15: As Row 7.
Row 16: As Row 6.
Row 17: As Row 5.
Row 18: As Row 4.
Row 19: As Row 3.
Row 20: As Row 2.

PANEL B
(worked over 14 sts)
Row 1 (RS): K2, p2, k6, p2, k2.
Row 2: P2, k2, p6, k2, p2.
Row 3: K2, p2, C6F, p2, k2.
Row 4: P2, k2, p6, k2, p2.
Rows 5–8: Rep Rows 1 and 2 twice more.

PANEL C
(worked over 14 sts)
Row 1 (RS): K2, p2, k6, p2, k2.
Row 2: P2, k2, p6, k2, p2.
Row 3: K2, p2, C6B, p2, k2.
Row 4: P2, k2, p6, k2, p2.
Rows 5–8: Rep Rows 1 and 2 twice more.

BACK
With size 3 needles, cast on 93 (100, 114, 121) sts.
Row 1: K3, *K1B, p2, k4; rep from * to last 6 sts, K1B, p2, k3.
Row 2: P3, *k2, P1B, p4, rep from * to last 6 sts, k2, P1B, p3.
Row 3: K3, *T2F, p1, k4; rep from * to last 6 sts, T2F, p1, k3.
Row 4: P3, *k1, P1B, k1, p4, rep from * to last 6 sts, k1, P1B, k1, p3.
Row 5: K3, *p1, T2F, k4; rep from * to last 6 sts, T2F, p1, k3.
Row 6: P3, *P1B, k2, p4; rep from * to last 6 sts, P1B, k2, p3.
Row 7: K3, *p1, T2B, k4; rep from * to last 6 sts, T2B, p1, k3.
Row 8: P3, *P1B, k2, p4; rep from * to last 6 sts, P1B, k2, p3.
Row 9: K3, *T2B, p1, k4; rep from * to last 6 sts, T2B, p1, k3.
Rep Rows 2–9 three times more and Row 2 again.
Inc row: K to end, increasing 3 (6, 2, 5) sts evenly across row—96 (106, 116, 126) sts.
Change to size 6 needles and patt. Beg with a p row, cont in st st until Back measures 17" (17¼", 18", 18½") [43 (44, 46, 47)cm] from cast-on edge, ending with a k row.
Inc row: P29 (32, 37, 40), m1pw, p2, m1pw, p34 (38, 38, 42), m1pw, p2,

m1pw, p29 (32, 37, 40)—100 (110, 120, 130) sts.
Cont in yoke patt.
Row 1: P1 (0, 1, 0), [k1, p1] 2 (3, 5, 6) times, work across 1st row of Panel A, p1, [k1, p1] 2 (3, 3, 4) times, work across 1st row of Panel B, p1, [k1, p1] 2 (3, 3, 4) times, work across 1st row of Panel A, p1, [k1, p1] 2 (3, 3, 4) times, work across 1st row of Panel C, p1, [k1, p1] 2 (3, 3, 4) times, work across 1st row of Panel A, [p1, k1] 2 (3, 5, 6) times, p1 (0, 1, 0).
Row 2: P1 (0, 1, 0), [k1, p1] 2 (3, 5, 6) times, work across 2nd row of Panel A, p1, [k1, p1] 2 (3, 3, 4) times, work across 2nd row of Panel C, p1, [k1, p1] 2 (3, 3, 4) times, work across 2nd row of Panel A, p1, [k1, p1] 2 (3, 3, 4) times, work across 2nd row of Panel B, p1, [k1, p1] 2 (3, 3, 4) times, work across 2nd row of Panel A, [p1, k1] 2 (3, 5, 6) times, p1 (0, 1, 0).
Row 3: P1 (0, 1, 0), [k1, p1] 2 (3, 5, 6) times, work across 3rd row of Panel A, p1, [k1, p1] 2 (3, 3, 4) times, work across 3rd row of Panel B, p1, [k1,

p1] 2 (3, 3, 4) times, work across 3rd row of Panel A, p1, [k1, p1] 2 (3, 3, 4) times, work across 3rd row of Panel C, p1, [k1, p1] 2 (3, 3, 4) times, work across 3rd row of Panel A, [p1, k1] 2 (3, 5, 6) times, p1 (0, 1, 0).
Row 4: P1 (0, 1, 0), [k1, p1] 2 (3, 5, 6) times, work across 4th row of Panel A, p1, [k1, p1] 2 (3, 3, 4) times, work across 4th row of Panel C, p1, [k1, p1] 2 (3, 3, 4) times, work across 4th row of Panel A, p1, [k1, p1] 2 (3, 3, 4) times, work across 4th row of panel B, p1, [k1, p1] 2 (3, 3, 4) times, work across 4th row of Panel A, [p1, k1] 2 (3, 5, 6) times, p1 (0, 1, 0).
These 4 rows set the position for the patt panels and form the moss st.
Cont even until Back measures 29¼" (30", 30¾", 31½") [74 (76, 78, 80)cm] from cast-on edge, ending with a wrong-side row.

Shape neck
Next row: Patt 39 (43, 46, 50), turn and work on these sts for 1st side of neck shaping.

Bind off 2 (4, 4, 6) sts at beg of next row.
Work 1 row.
Bind off 2 sts at beg of next and foll alt row—33 (35, 38, 40) sts.
Work 2 rows.

Shape shoulder
Bind off 16 (17, 19, 20) sts at beg of next row.
Work 1 row.
Bind off rem 17 (18, 19, 20) sts.
With right side facing, rejoin yarn to rem sts, bind off center 22 (24, 28, 30) sts, patt to end.
Complete to match 1st side.

FRONT
Work as given for Back until Front measures 25¾" (26½", 26¾", 27½") [65 (67, 68, 70)cm] from cast-on edge, ending with a wrong-side row.

Shape neck
Next row: Patt 44 (48, 51, 55), turn and work on these sts for 1st side of neck shaping.
Bind off 2 sts at beg of next and foll alt row.
Dec 1 st at neck edge of every row until 33 (35, 38, 40) sts rem.
Cont even until Front measures same as Back to shoulder, ending at armhole edge.

Shape shoulder
Bind off 16 (17, 19, 20) sts at beg of next row.
Work 1 row.
Bind off rem 17 (18, 19, 20) sts.
With right side facing, slip center 12 (14, 18, 20) sts onto a spare needle, rejoin yarn to rem sts, patt to end.
Complete to match 1st side.

SLEEVES (MAKE 2)
With size 3 needles, cast on 37 (37, 44, 44) sts.
Row 1: K3, *K1B, p2, k4; rep from * to last 6 sts, K1B, p2, k3.
Row 2: P3, *k2, P1B, p4, rep from * to last 6 sts, k2, P1B, p3.

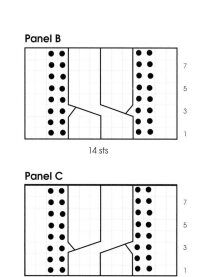

Panel A

14 sts

Panel B

14 sts

Panel C

14 sts

KEY
⬛ = p on RS, k on WS   ⬜ = k on RS, p on WS

⬛⧄⬜ = C6B   ⬛⧄⬜ = C6F

Row 3: K3, *T2F, p1, k4; rep from * to last 6 sts, T2F, p1, k3.
Row 4: P3, *k1, P1B, k1; p4; rep from * to last 6 sts, k1, P1B, k1, p3.
Row 5: K3, *p1, T2F, k4; rep from * to last 6 sts, T2F, p1, k3.
Row 6: P3, *P1B, k2, p4; rep from * to last 6 sts, P1B, k2, p3.
Row 7: K3, *p1, T2B, k4; rep from * to last 6 sts, T2B, p1, k3.
Row 8: P3, *P1B, k2, p4; rep from * to last 6 sts, P1B, k2, p3.
Row 9: K3, *T2B, p1, k4; rep from * to last 6 sts, T2B, p1, k3.
Rep Rows 2–9 once more and Row 2 again, dec 1 st at center of row on Small and Medium sizes only—36 (36, 44, 44) sts.
Change to size 6 needles and patt. Beg with a k row, cont in st st.
Work 4 rows.
Inc row: K3, m1, k to last 3 sts, m1, k3.
Work 3 rows.
Rep the last 4 rows until there are 70 (70, 78, 78) sts, ending with an inc row.
Inc row: P14 (14, 18, 18), m1pw, p2, m1pw, p38, m1pw, p2, m1pw, p14 (14, 18, 18)—74 (74, 82, 82) sts.
Cont in patt.
Row 1: K2 (2, 6, 6), p1, [k1, p1] 3 times, work across 1st row of Panel B, p1, [k1, p1] 3 times, work across 1st row of Panel A, p1, [k1, p1] 3 times, work across 1st row of Panel C, p1, [k1, p1] 3 times, k2 (2, 6, 6).
Row 2: P3 (3, 7, 7), [k1, p1] 3 times, work across 2nd row of Panel C, p1, [k1, p1] 3 times, work across 2nd row of Panel A, p1, [k1, p1] 3 times, work across 2nd row of Panel B, [p1, k1] 3 times, p3 (3, 7, 7).
These 2 rows set the position for the patt panels and form the moss st.
Cont in patt as set, inc 1 st at each end of next and every foll 4th row until there are 104 (104, 112, 112) sts, working 1st 12 (12, 8, 8) sts into Panel A, and remaining 3 (3, 7, 7) sts in moss st.

Work even until Sleeve measures 22" (22½", 22⅔", 23¼")" [56 (57, 58, 59)cm] from cast-on edge, ending with a wrong-side row.
Bind off.

NECKBAND
Join right shoulder seam.
With right side facing and size 3 needles, pick up and k23 (23, 24, 25) sts down left front neck, k12 (14, 18, 20) sts from front neck holder, pick up and k23 (24, 24, 24) sts up right front neck, 10 (12, 12, 14) sts down right back neck, 22 (24, 28, 30) sts across center back neck, k10 (12, 12, 14) sts up left side of back neck—100 (109, 118, 127) sts.
Rep Rows 2 and 9 of welt twice, then Row 2 again.
Bind off.

FINISHING
Join left shoulder and neckband seam. Sew on Sleeves. Join side and sleeve seams.

whitby sweater

Taking its name from a Yorkshire fishing village, this is possibly the most copied sweater design in knitting history, having found its way into many other designers' collections as well. A stunning picture of our original Whitby is featured in the centenary edition of *Vogue*.

Sizes S (M, L, XL)

Measurements after Washing
Chest: 37¾" (41¾", 45¾", 49¾") [96 (106, 116, 126)cm]
Length to shoulder: 25½" (26½", 27¼", 28") [65 (67, 69, 71)cm]
Sleeve length: 19" (19¼", 19¾", 20") [48 (49, 50, 51)cm]

Materials
- 20 (21, 23, 24) balls Elann Den-M-Nit (100% cotton, 1¾ oz [50g], 101 yd [92m]) in Mid Indigo
- Size 5 (3.75mm) needles
- Size 6 (4mm) needles
- Cable needle
- Thread in a contrasting color

Gauge
20 sts and 28 rows = 4" (10cm) square in st st using size 6 needles before washing.

Abbreviations and Techniques
Refer to pages 18–19.

PANEL A
(worked over 16 sts)
Row 1 (RS): K2, p2, k8, p2, k2.
Row 2: P2, k2, p8, k2, p2.
Row 3: K2, p2, C8B, p2, k2.
Row 4: P2, k2, p8, k2, p2.

PANEL B
(worked over 18 sts)
Row 1 (RS): P7, C4B, p7.
Row 2: K7, p4, k7.
Row 3: P6, C3B, C3F, p6.
Row 4: K6, p6, k6.
Row 5: P5, C3B, k2, C3F, p5.
Row 6: K5, p8, k5.
Row 7: P4, T3B, C4B, T3F, p4.
Row 8: K4, p2, k1, p4, k1, p2, k4.
Row 9: P3, T3B, p1, k4, p1, T3F, p3.
Row 10: K3, p2, k2, p4, k2, p2, k3.
Row 11: P2, T3B, p2, C4B, p2, T3F, p2.
Row 12: K2, p2, k3, p4, k3, p2, k2.
Row 13: P1, T3B, p3, k4, p3, T3F, p1.
Row 14: K1, p2, k4, p4, k4, p2, k1.
Row 15: P1, k2, p4, C4B, p4, k2, p1.
Row 16: As Row 14.
Row 17: P1, T3F, p3, k4, p3, T3B, p1.
Row 18: As Row 12.
Row 19: P2, T3F, p2, C4B, p2, T3B, p2.
Row 20: As Row 10.
Row 21: P3, T3F, p1, k4, p1, T3B, p3.
Row 22: As Row 8.
Row 23: P4, T3F, C4B, T3B, p4.
Row 24: As Row 6.
Row 25: P5, T3F, k2, T3B, p5.
Row 26: As Row 4.
Row 27: P6, T3F, T3B, p6.
Row 28: K7, p4, k7.

PANEL C
(worked over 23 sts)
Row 1 (RS): [P2, k2] twice, p7, [k2, p2] twice.
Row 2: [K2, yp2] twice, k7, [yp2, k2] twice.
Row 3: [P2, k2] twice, p3, m1, [k1, p1, k1] in next st, m1, p3, [k2, p2] twice—27 sts.
Row 4: [K2, yp2] twice, k3, p2, k1, p2, k3, [yp2, k2] twice.
Row 5: P2, k2, p2, T3F, T4B, p1, T4F, T3B, p2, k2, p2.
Row 6: K2, yp2, k3, p4, k5, p4, k3, yp2, k2.
Row 7: P2, k2, p3, C4B, p5, C4B, p3, k2, p2.
Row 8: As Row 6.
Row 9: P2, T3F, T4B, T4F, p1, T4B, T4F, T3B, p2.
Row 10: K3, p4, k4, p2, k1, p2, k4, p4, k3.
Row 11: P3, C4F, p4, CR5, p4, C4F, p3.
Row 12: As Row 10.
Row 13: P1, T4B, T4F, T4B, p1, T4F, T4B, T4F, p1.
Row 14: K1, p2, k4, p4, k5, p4, k4, p2, k1.
Row 15: P1, k2, p4, C4B, p5, C4B, p4, k2, p1.
Row 16: As Row 14.
Row 17: P1, T4F, T4B, T4F, p1, T4B, T4F, T4B, p1.

Panel A

16 sts

Panel B

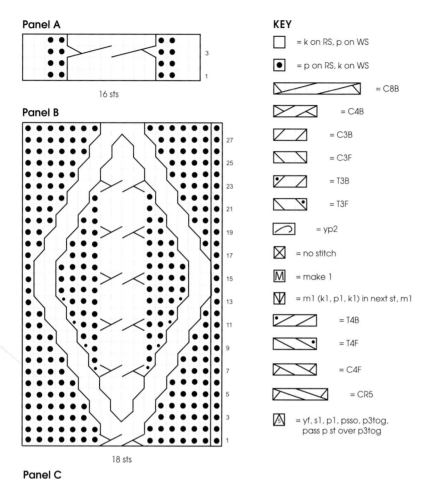

18 sts

Panel C

23 sts increasing to 27 sts

KEY

☐ = k on RS, p on WS

⊡ = p on RS, k on WS

= C8B

= C4B

= C3B

= C3F

= T3B

= T3F

= yp2

⊠ = no stitch

Ⓜ = make 1

= m1 (k1, p1, k1) in next st, m1

= T4B

= T4F

= C4F

= CR5

= yf, s1, p1, psso, p3tog, pass p st over p3tog

Row 18: As Row 10.
Row 19: P3, C4F, p4, CR5, p4, C4F, p3.
Row 20: As Row 10.
Row 21: P2, T3B, T4F, T4B, p1, T4F, T4B, T3F, p2.
Row 22: As Row 6.
Row 23: P2, k2, p3, C4B, p5, C4B, p3, k2, p2.
Row 24: As Row 6.
Row 25: P2, k2, p2, T3B, T4F, p1, T4B, T3F, p2, k2, p2.
Row 26: [K2, yp2] twice, k3, yf, sl 1, p1, psso, p3tog, pass last p st over the p3tog, k3, [yp2, k2] twice.
Row 27: [P2, k2] twice, p7, [k2, p2] twice.
Row 28: [K2, yp2] twice, k7, [yp2, k2] twice.

BACK

With size 5 needles, cast on 122 (130, 142, 150) sts.

S/M sizes only
Rib Row 1: K2, *p2, k2; rep from * to end.
Rib Row 2: P2, *k2, p2; rep from * to end.
These 2 rows form the rib.

L/XL sizes only
Rib Row 1: P2, *k2, p2; rep from * to end.
Rib Row 2: K2, *p2, k2; rep from * to end.
These 2 rows form the rib.

All sizes
Work a further 21 rows.
Inc row: Rib 10 (14, 20, 24), m1, rib 2, m1, rib 30, m1, rib 2, m1, rib 17, m1, rib 17, m1, rib 2, m1, rib 30, m1, rib 2, m1, rib 10 (14, 30, 24)—131 (139, 151, 159) sts.
Change to size 6 needles and patt.
Row 1 (RS): [K1, p1] 2 (4, 7, 9) times, work across 1st row of Panels A, B, A, C, A, B, and A, [p1, k1] 2 (4, 7, 9) times.

Row 2: [P1, k1] 2 (4, 7, 9) times, work across 2nd row of Panels A, B, A, C, A, B, and A, [k1, p1] 2 (4, 7, 9) times.
Row 3: [P1, k1] 2 (4, 7, 9) times, work across 3rd row of Panels A, B, A, C, A, B, and A, [k1, p1] 2 (4, 7, 9) times.
Row 4 (RS): [K1, p1] 2 (4, 7, 9) times, work across 1st row of Panels A, B, A, C, A, B, and A, [p1, k1] 2 (4, 7, 9) times.
These 4 rows set the position for the patt panels and form the double moss st.
Cont in patt until Back measures 19" (19¼", 20", 20½") [48 (49, 51, 52)cm] from cast-on edge, ending with wrong-side row.

Shape armholes
Bind off 3 (4, 6, 8) sts at beg of next 2 rows—125 (131, 139, 143) sts.
Cont even until Back measures 29¼" (30", 30¾", 31½") [74 (76, 78, 80)cm] from cast-on edge, ending with a wrong-side row.

Shape neck
Next row: Patt 42 (44, 47, 48), turn and work on these sts for 1st side of neck shaping.
Dec 1 st at neck edge of next 4 rows—38 (40, 43, 44) sts.
Work 3 rows.

Shape shoulder
Bind off 19 (20, 21, 22) sts at beg of next row.
Work 1 row.
Bind off rem 19 (20, 22, 22) sts.
With right side facing, rejoin yarn to rem sts, bind off center 41 (43, 45, 47) sts, patt to end.
Complete to match 1st side.

FRONT
Work as given for Back until Front measures 25¾" (26½", 26¾", 27½") [65 (67, 68, 70)cm] from cast-on edge, ending with a wrong-side row.

Shape neck
Next row: Patt 47 (49, 52, 53), turn and work on these sts for 1st side of neck shaping.
Dec 1 st at neck edge of every row until 38 (40, 43, 44) sts rem.
Cont even until Front measures same as Back to shoulder, ending at armhole edge.

Shape shoulder
Bind off 19 (20, 21, 22) sts at beg of next row.
Work 1 row.
Bind off rem 19 (20, 22, 22) sts.
With right side facing, slip center 31 (33, 35, 37) sts onto a spare needle, rejoin yarn to rem sts, patt to end.
Complete to match 1st side.

SLEEVES (MAKE 2)
With size 5 needles, cast on 50 (50, 54, 54) sts.

S/M sizes only
Rib Row 1: P2, *k2, p2; rep from * to end.
Rib Row 2: K2, *p2, k2; rep from * to end.

L/XL sizes only
Rib Row 1: K2, *p2, k2; rep from * to end.
Rib Row 2: P2, *k2, p2; rep from * to end.
These 2 rows form the rib.

All sizes
Work a further 17 rows.
Inc row: Rib 8 (8, 10, 10), m1, rib 2, m1, rib 30, m1, rib 2, m1, rib 8 (8, 10, 10)—54 (54, 58, 58) sts.
Change to size 6 needles and patt.
Row 1 (RS): K0 (0, 2, 2), p2, work across 1st row of Panels A, B, and A, p2, k0 (0, 2, 2).
Row 2: P0 (0, 2, 2), k2, work across 2nd row of Panels A, B, and A, k2, p0 (0, 2, 2).
Row 3: K0 (0, 2, 2), p2, work across 3rd row of Panels A, B, and A, p2, k0 (0, 2, 2).
Row 4: P0 (0, 2, 2), k2, work across 1st row of Panels A, B, and A, k2, p0 (0, 2, 2).
These 4 rows set the position for the patt Panels.
Inc and work into Panel A, *but only keep 1 k2 between cables* 1 st at each end of the next and every foll 4th row until there are 112 (116, 120, 124) sts, working 1st 12 (12, 10, 10) sts into Panel A and rem sts in double moss st.
Work even until sleeve measures 22" (22½", 22⅔", 23¼") [56 (57, 58, 59)cm] from cast-on edge, ending with a wrong-side row.
Mark each end of last row with a colored thread.
Work a further 6 (8, 10, 12) rows.
Bind off.

NECKBAND
Join right shoulder seam.
With right side facing and size 5 needles, pick up and k24 (24, 26, 26) sts down left Front neck, k31 (33, 35, 37) sts from Front neck holder, pick up and k24 (24, 26, 26) sts up right Front neck, 6 sts down right Back neck, 41 (43, 45, 47) sts across center Back neck, pick up and k6 sts up left side of Back neck—122 (126, 134, 138) sts.
Next row: P2, *k2, p2; rep from * to end.
Next row: K2, *p2, k2; rep from * to end.
Rep the last 2 rows 14 times more.
Bind off in rib.

FINISHING
Join left shoulder and neckband seam.
Sew on Sleeves, sewing rows above colored threads to sts bind off at underarm. Join side and sleeve seams.

newlyn jacket

Artwork has had a lot of success with this style over the years. Our original Artwork design had a much larger shape to it; this version is scaled down for a more compact, contemporary fit.

PANEL A
(worked over 11 sts)
Row 1 (RS): P3, T2B, K1B, T2F, p3.
Row 2: K3, [P1B, k1] twice, P1B, k3.
Row 3: P2, T2B, p1, K1B, p1, T2F, p2.
Row 4: [K2, P1B] 3 times, k2.
Row 5: P1, T2B, p1, [K1B] 3 times, p1, T2F, p1.
Row 6: K1, P1B, k2, [p1b] 3 times, k2, P1B, k1.

PANEL B
(worked over 6 sts)
Row 1 (RS): P1, k4, p1.
Row 2: K1, p4, k1.
Row 3: P1, C4F, p1.
Row 4: K1, p4, k1.

PANEL C
(worked over 6 sts)
Row 1 (RS): P1, k4, p1.
Row 2: K1, p4, k1.
Row 3: P1, C4B, p1.
Row 4: K1, p4, k1.

PANEL D
(worked over 18 sts)
Row 1 (RS): P7, C4B, p7.
Row 2: K7, p4, k7.
Row 3: P6, C3B, C3F, p6.
Row 4: K6, p6, k6.
Row 5: P5, C3B, k2, C3F, p5.
Row 6: K5, p8, k5.
Row 7: P4, T3B, C4B, T3F, p4.
Row 8: K4, p2, k1, p4, k1, p2, k4.
Row 9: P3, T3B, p1, k4, p1, T3F, p3.
Row 10: K3, p2, k2, p4, k2, p2, k3.

Row 11: P2, T3B, p2, C4B, p2, T3F, p2.
Row 12: K2, p2, k3, p4, k3, p2, k2.
Row 13: P1, T3B, p3, k4, p3, T3F, p1.
Row 14: K1, p2, k4, p4, k4, p2, k1.
Row 15: P1, k2, p4, C4B, p4, k2, p1.
Row 16: As Row 14.
Row 17: P1, T3F, p3, k4, p3, T3B, p1.
Row 18: As Row 12.
Row 19: P2, T3F, p2, C4B, p2, T3B, p2.
Row 20: As Row 10.
Row 21: P3, T3F, p1, k4, p1, T3B, p3.
Row 22: As Row 8.
Row 23: P4, T3F, C4B, T3B, p4.
Row 24: As Row 6.
Row 25: P5, T3F, k2, T3B, p5.
Row 26: As Row 4.
Row 27: P6, T3F, T3B, p6.
Row 28: K7, p4, k7.

BACK
With size 5 needles, cast on 123 (131, 139, 151, 163, 175) sts.
Moss st row: K1, *p1, k1; rep from * to end.
This row forms the moss st.
Work a further 12 rows.
Inc row: Moss st 11 (15, 19, 25, 31, 37), m1, moss st 20, m1, moss st 2, m1, moss st 21, m1, moss st 16, m1, moss st 20, m1, moss st 2, m1, moss st, 21, m1, moss st 10 (14, 18, 24, 30, 36)—131 (139, 147, 159, 171, 183) sts.
Change to size 6 needles and patt.
Row 1 (RS): Moss st 8 (12, 16, 22, 28, 34), work across 1st row of Panels

Sizes
XS (S, M, L, XL, XXL)

Measurements after Washing
Bust: 35" (38", 41", 45", 49", 54") [89 (97, 104, 114, 124, 37)cm]
Length to shoulder: 25" (25½", 26½", 26¾", 27½", 28¼") [64 (65, 67, 68, 70, 72)cm]
Sleeve length: 17¼" (17¼", 17¾", 17¾", 18", 18") [44 (44, 45, 45, 46, 46)cm]

Materials
▸ 20 (21, 23, 24, 26, 28) balls Elann Den-M-Nit (100% cotton, 1¾ oz [50g], 101 yd [92m]) in Ecru
▸ Size 5 (3.75mm) needles
▸ Size 6 (4mm) needles
▸ Stitch holder
▸ Cable needle
▸ 9 buttons
▸ Sewing needle and thread

Gauge
20 sts and 28 rows = 4" (10cm) square in st st using size 6 needles before washing.

Abbreviations and Techniques
Refer to pages 18–19.

The old harbor in Newlyn.

B, A, D, A, C, A, B, A, D, A, and C, moss st 8 (12, 16, 22, 28, 34).

Row 2: Moss st 8 (12, 16, 22, 28, 34), work across 2nd row of Panels C, A, D, A, B, A, C, A, D, A, and B, moss st 8 (12, 16, 22, 28, 34).

Row 3: Moss st 8 (12, 16, 22, 28, 34), work across 3rd row of Panels B, A, D, A, C, A, B, A, D, A, and C, moss st 8 (12, 16, 20, 28, 34).

Row 4: Moss st 8 (12, 16, 22, 28, 34), work across 4th row of Panels C, A,

D, A, B, A, C, A, D, A, and B, moss st 8 (12, 16, 22, 28, 34).

These 4 rows set the position for the patt panels.

Cont in patt until Back measures 9" (9", 9", 9½", 9½", 9½") [23 (23, 23, 24, 24, 24)cm] from cast-on edge, ending with a wrong-side row.

Change to size 5 needles (to draw the waist in slightly) and work a further 4¾" (12cm).

Change to size 6 needles.

Cont in patt until Back measures 20½" (20½", 20¾", 20¾", 21¼", 21¾") [52 (52, 53, 53, 54, 55)cm] from cast-on edge, ending with a wrong-side row.

Shape armholes

Bind off 4 (6, 8, 11, 14, 17) sts at beg of next 2 rows—123 (127, 131, 137, 143, 149) sts.

Cont even until Back measures 29½" (30¼", 31", 31½", 32¼", 33") [75

(77, 79, 80, 82, 84)cm] from cast-on edge, ending with a wrong-side row.

Shape shoulders

Bind off 20 (21, 21, 22, 23, 24) sts at beg of next 2 rows and 21 (21, 22, 23, 24, 25) sts at beg of foll 2 rows.
Bind off rem 41 (43, 45, 47, 49, 51) sts.

POCKET LININGS (MAKE 2)

With size 6 needles, cast on 24 (24, 26, 26, 28, 30) sts.
Beg with a k row, cont in st st until work measures 6¾" (17cm) from cast-on edge, ending with a k row.
Next row: P11 (11, 12, 12), m1pw, p2, m1pw, p11 (11, 12, 12)—26 (26, 28, 28, 30, 32) sts. Leave on spare needle.

LEFT FRONT

With size 5 needles, cast on 67 (71, 75, 81, 87, 93) sts.
Moss st row: P1, *k1, p1; rep from * to end.
This row forms the moss st.
Work a further 12 rows.
Inc row: Moss st 11 (15, 19, 25, 31, 37), m1, moss st 20, m1, moss st 2, m1, moss st 21, m1, moss st 13—71 (75, 79, 85, 91, 97) sts.
Change to size 6 needles and patt.
Row 1 (RS): Moss st 8 (12, 16, 22, 28, 34), work across 1st row of Panels B, A, D, A, and C, moss st 11.
Row 2: Moss st 11, work across 2nd row of Panels C, A, D, A, and B, moss st 8 (12, 16, 22, 28, 34).

Row 3: Moss st 8 (12, 16, 22, 28, 34), work across 3rd row of Panels B, A, D, A, and C, moss st 11.
Row 4: Moss st 11, work across row 4 of Panels C, A, D, A, B, moss st 8 (12, 16, 22, 28, 34).
These 4 rows set the position for the patt panels.
Cont in patt until Front measures 6¾" (17cm) from cast-on edge, ending with a wrong-side row.

Place pocket

Next row: Patt 21 (25, 28, 34, 39, 44), slip next 26 (26, 28, 28, 30, 32) sts onto a holder, patt across 26 (26, 28, 28, 30, 32) sts of 1st pocket lining, patt to end.
Cont in patt until Front measures 9" (9", 9", 9½", 9½", 9½") [23 (23, 23, 24, 24, 24)cm] in from cast-on edge, ending with a wrong-side row.
Change to size 5 needles and work a further 4¾" (12cm).
Change to size 6 needles.
Cont in patt until Front measures 20½" (20½", 20¾", 20¾", 21¼", 21¾") [52 (52, 53, 53, 54, 55)cm] from cast-on edge, ending with a wrong-side row.

Shape armhole

Bind off 4 (6, 8, 11, 14, 17) sts at beg of next row—67 (69, 71, 74, 77, 80) sts.
Cont in patt until Front measures 26¾" (27½", 28", 28¼", 28½", 29")

[68 (70, 71, 72, 73, 74)cm] from cast-on edge, ending with a wrong-side row.

Shape neck

Next row: Patt to last 16 sts, place these sts on a stitch holder, turn.
Next row: Patt to end.
Dec 1 st at neck edge on every row until 41 (42, 43, 45, 47, 49) sts rem.
Cont even until Front measures same as Back to shoulder shaping, ending at armhole edge.

Shape shoulder

Bind off 20 (21, 21, 22, 23, 24) sts at beg of next row.
Work 1 row.
Bind off rem 21 (21, 22, 23, 24, 25) sts.

RIGHT FRONT

Mark positions on Left Front for 9 buttons, the first one ¾" (2cm) from cast-on edge, the last one ½" (13mm) from neck, and 7 spaced evenly between.
With size 5 needles, cast on 67 (71, 75, 81, 87, 93) sts.
Moss st row: P1, *k1, p1; rep from * to end.
This row forms the moss st.
Work a further 5 rows.
Buttonhole Row 1: Moss st 4, ptog, y2rn, k2tog, moss st to end.
Buttonhole Row 2: Moss st to end, working twice in y2rn.
Work a further 5 rows.
Inc row: Moss st 13, m1, moss st 20, m1, moss st 2, m1, moss st 21, m1, moss st 11 (15, 19, 25, 31, 37)—71 (75, 79, 85, 91, 97) sts.
Change to size 6 needles and patt.
Row 1 (RS): Moss st 11, work across 1st row of Panels B, A, D, A, and C, moss st 8 (12, 16, 22, 28, 34).
Row 2: Moss st 8 (12, 16, 22, 28, 34), work across 2nd row of Panels C, A, D, A, and B, moss st 11.
Row 3: Moss st 11, work across 3rd row of Panels B, A, D, A, and C, moss st 8 (12, 16, 22, 28, 34).

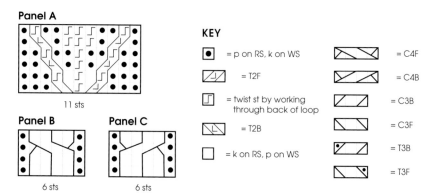

Panel A

11 sts

KEY

⊡ = p on RS, k on WS
◿ = T2F
⌐⌐ = twist st by working through back of loop
◺◹ = T2B
☐ = k on RS, p on WS

⟋⟍ = C4F
⟋⟍ = C4B
⟋ = C3B
⟍ = C3F
⟍ = T3B
⟋ = T3F

Panel B
6 sts

Panel C
6 sts

Panel D = is same as Panel B from the Whitby Sweater (page 30)

Row 4: Moss st 8 (12, 16, 22, 28, 34), work across 4th row of Panels C, A, D, A, and B, moss st 11.

These 4 rows set the position for the patt panels.

Cont in patt until Front measures 6¾" (17cm) from cast-on edge, ending with a wrong-side row.

Place pocket

Next row: Patt 24 (24, 23, 23, 22, 21), slip next 26 (26, 28, 28, 30, 32) sts onto a holder, patt across 26 (26, 28, 28, 30, 32) sts of second pocket lining, patt to end.

Cont in patt until Front measures 9" (9", 9", 9½", 9½", 9½") [23 (23, 23, 24, 24, 24)cm] from cast-on edge, ending with a wrong-side row.

Change to size 5 needles and work an additional 4¾" (12cm).

Change to size 6 needles.

Cont in patt until Front measures 20½" (20½", 20¾", 20¾", 21¼", 21¾")" [52 (52, 53, 53, 54, 55)cm] from cast-on edge, ending with a right-side row.

Shape armhole

Bind off 4 (6, 8, 11, 14, 17) sts at beg of next row—67 (69, 71, 74, 77, 80) sts.

Cont in patt until Front measures 26¾" (27½", 28", 28¼", 28½", 29") [68 (70, 71, 72, 73, 74)cm] from cast-on edge, ending with WS row.

Shape neck

Next row: Patt 16 sts, place these sts on a stitch holder, patt to end.

Next row: Patt to end.

Dec 1 st at neck edge on every row until 41 (42, 43, 45, 47, 49) sts rem.

Cont even until Front measures same as Back to shoulder shaping, ending at armhole edge.

Shape shoulder

Bind off 20 (21, 21, 22, 23, 24) sts at beg of next row.

Work 1 row.

Bind off rem 21 (21, 22, 23, 24, 25) sts.

SLEEVES (MAKE 2)

With size 5 needles, cast on 52 (56, 60, 64, 72, 80) sts.

Moss st Row 1: *P1, k1; rep from * to end.

Moss st Row 2: *K1, p1; rep from * to end.

These 2 rows form the moss st.

Work a further 11 rows.

Inc row: Moss st 5 (7, 9, 11, 15, 19), m1, moss st 20, m1, moss st 2, m1, moss st 21, m1, moss st 4 (6, 8, 10, 14, 18)—56 (60, 64, 68, 76, 84) sts.

Change to size 6 needles and patt.

Row 1 (RS): Moss st 2 (4, 6, 8, 12, 16), work across 1st row of Panels B, A, D, A, and C, moss st 2 (4, 6, 8, 12, 16).

Row 2: Moss st 2 (4, 6, 8, 12, 16), work across 2nd row of Panels C, A, D, A, and B, moss st 2 (4, 6, 8, 12, 16).

Row 3: Moss st 2 (4, 6, 8, 12, 16), work across 3rd row of Panels B, A, D, A, and C, moss st 2 (4, 6, 8, 12, 16).

Row 4: Moss st 2 (4, 6, 8, 12, 16), work across 4th row of Panels C, A, D, A, and B, moss st 2 (4, 6, 8, 12, 16).

These 4 rows set the position for the patt panels.

Inc and work into moss st 1 st at each end of the next and every foll 7th row until there are 92 (96, 100, 104, 112, 120) sts.

Work even until Sleeve measures 20" (20", 20½", 20½", 21", 21") [51 (51, 52, 52, 53, 53)cm] from cast-on edge, ending with a wrong-side row.

Mark each end of last row with a colored thread.

Work a further 6 (8, 10, 12, 16, 20) rows.

Bind off.

COLLAR

Join shoulder seams.

With right side facing and size 5 needles, slip 16 sts from right Front neck holder onto a needle, pick up and k25 (25, 26, 26, 28, 28) sts up right Front neck, cast on 37 (39, 41, 43, 47, 51) sts, pick up and k25 (25, 26, 26, 28, 28) sts down left Front neck, then k5, moss st 11 sts from left Front holder—119 (121, 125, 127, 135, 139) sts.

Next row: Moss st to end.

Next 2 rows: Moss st to last 38 sts, turn.

Next 2 rows: Moss st to last 34 sts, turn.

Next 2 rows: Moss st to last 30 sts, turn.

Next 2 rows: Moss st to last 26 sts, turn.

Next 2 rows: Moss st to last 22 sts, turn.

Next 2 rows: Moss st to last 18 sts, turn.

Next row: Moss st to end.

Next 2 rows: Cast off 6 sts at beg of next 2 rows.

Change to size 6 needles.

Cont in moss st across all sts for an additional 4" (10cm).

Bind off in moss st.

POCKET TOPS

With size 5 needles and right side facing, slip 26 (26, 28, 28, 30, 32) sts onto a needle.

Row 1: K10 (10, 11, 11, 12, 13), k2tog, k2, k2tog, k10 (10, 11, 11, 12, 13)—24 (24, 26, 26, 28, 30) sts.

Moss st Row 1: *P1, k1; rep from * to end.

Moss st Row 2: *K1, p1; rep from * to end.

Work a further 6 rows.

Bind off.

FINISHING

Sew on Sleeves. Join side and sleeve seams. Sew down Pocket Linings and pocket tops. Sew on buttons.

romney marsh smock

Sizes
1–2 years (3–4 years, 5–6 years, 7–8 years, 9–10 years)

Measurements after Washing
Chest: 26" (28¼", 30¾", 33", 35½") [66 (72, 78, 84, 90)cm]
Length: 13¾" (15¾", 17¾", 19¾", 21¾") [35 (40, 45, 50, 55)cm]
Sleeve length: 8¾" (10", 11", 12½", 13¾") [22 (25, 28, 32, 35)cm]

Materials
- 8 (10, 12, 14, 16) balls Elann Den-M-Nit (100% cotton, 1¾ oz [50g], 101 yd [92m]) in Pale Indigo
- Size 3 (3mm) needles
- Size 6 (4mm) needles
- Size 5 (3.75mm) needles
- Cable needle
- Sewing needle and thread

Gauge
20 sts and 28 rows = 4" (10cm) square in st st using size 6 needles before washing.

Abbreviations and Techniques
Refer to pages 18–19.

Named for a coastal region in Kent, this children's sweater is styled after a traditional fisherman's knit. For extra interest, we've added two side pockets, one on each side. The original sweaters did sometimes include one pocket, called a fob, where the fishermen would keep their watches—if they were lucky enough to own one!

PANEL A
(worked over 11 sts)
Row 1 (WS): K2, P1B, [k1, P1B] 3 times, k2.
Row 2: P2, K1B, [p1, K1B] 3 times, p2.
Row 3: As Row 1.
Row 4: P2, CR7L, p2.
Rows 5–14: Rep Rows 1 and 2 five times more.

PANEL B
(worked over 13 sts)
Row 1 (WS): P13.
Row 2: K2, FC2, k8.
Row 3 and every foll odd row: P13.
Row 4: K3, FC2, k7.
Row 6: K4, FC2, k6.
Row 8: K5, FC2, k5.
Row 10: K6, FC2, k4.
Row 12: K7, FC2, k3.
Row 14: K8, FC2, k2.
Row 16: K8, BC2, k2.
Row 18: K7, BC2, k3.
Row 20: K6, BC2, k4.
Row 22: K5, BC2, k5.
Row 24: K4, BC2, k6.
Row 26: K3, BC2, k7.
Row 28: K2, BC2, k8.

PANEL C
(worked over 33 sts)
Row 1 (WS): P33.
Row 2: K1, *LT, [RT] twice, k3, [LT] twice, RT, k1; rep from * once more.
Row 3 and every foll odd row: P33.

Row 4: K2, *LT, [RT] twice, k1, [LT] twice, RT, k3; rep from * once more, ending 2nd rep k2.
Row 6: K1, *[LT] twice, RT, k3, LT, [RT] twice, k1; rep from * once more.
Row 8: K2, *[LT] twice, RT, k1, LT, [RT] twice, k3; rep from * once more, ending 2nd rep k2.
Row 10: K1, *[LT] 3 times, k3, [RT] 3 times, k1; rep from * once more.
Row 12: K2, *[LT] 3 times, k1, [RT] 3 times, k3; rep from * once more, ending 2nd rep k2.
Row 14: As Row 10.
Row 16: As Row 8.
Row 18: As Row 6.
Row 20: As Row 4.
Row 22: As Row 2.
Row 24: K2, *[RT] 3 times, k1, [LT] 3 times, k3; rep from * once more, ending 2nd rep k2.
Row 26: K1, *[RT] 3 times, k3, [LT] 3 times, k1; rep from * once more.
Row 28: As Row 24.

PANEL D
(worked over 13 sts)
Row 1 (WS): P13.
Row 2: K8, BC2, k2.
Row 3 and every foll odd row: P13.
Row 4: K7, BC2, k3.
Row 6: K6, BC2, k4.
Row 8: K5, BC2, k5.
Row 10: K4, BC2, k6.
Row 12: K3, BC2, k7.
Row 14: K2, BC2, k8.

Row 16: K2, FC2, k8.
Row 18: K3, FC2, k7.
Row 20: K4, FC2, k6.
Row 22: K5, FC2, k5.
Row 24: K6, FC2, k4.
Row 26: K7, FC2, k3.
Row 28: K8, FC2, k2.

BACK

With size 3 needles, cast on 82 (82, 95, 95, 108) sts.
Row 1: K4, *p3, [K1B] 3 times, p3, k4; rep from * to end.
Row 2: P4, *k3, [P1B] 3 times, k3, p4; rep from * to end.
Row 3: K4, *p2, BC, K1B, FC, p2, k4; rep from * to end.
Row 4: P4, *k2, P1B, [k1, P1B] twice, k2, p4; rep from * to end.
Row 5: K4, *p1, BC, p1, K1B, p1, FC, p1, k4; rep from * to end.
Row 6: P4, *k1, p1B, [k2, P1B] twice, k1, p4; rep from * to end.
Row 7: K4, *BC, p2, K1B, p2, FC, k4; rep from * to end.
Row 8: P4, *k4, P1B, k4, p4; rep from * to end.
Rep these 8 rows 1 (1, 1, 2, 2) times more.
P3 rows, inc 3 (9, 2, 8, 1) sts evenly across last row—85 (91, 97, 103, 109) sts.
Change to size 6 needles and patt.

1–2/3–4/5–6 sizes only
Row 1: K2 (5, 8), work across 1st row of Panels D, A, C, A, and B, k2 (5, 8).
Row 2: P2 (5, 8), work across 2nd row of Panels B, A, C, A, and D, p2 (5, 8).
Row 3: K2 (5, 8), work across 3rd row of Panels D, A, C, A, and B, k2 (5, 8).
Row 4: P2 (5, 8), work across 4th row of Panels B, A, C, A, and D, p2 (5, 8).
These 4 rows set the patt for Panels A, B, C, and D.

7–8/9–10 sizes only
Row 1: K(0, 3), work across 1st row of Panels A, D, A, C, A, B, and A, k(0, 3).
Row 2: P(0, 3), work across 2nd row of Panels A, B, A, C, A, D, and A, p(0, 3)

Panel A

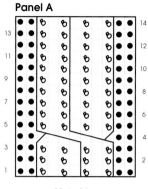

11 sts, 14 rows

KEY

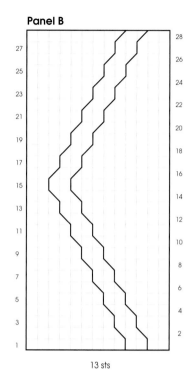

Panel B

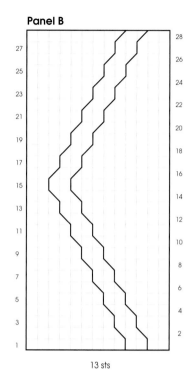

13 sts

Panel C

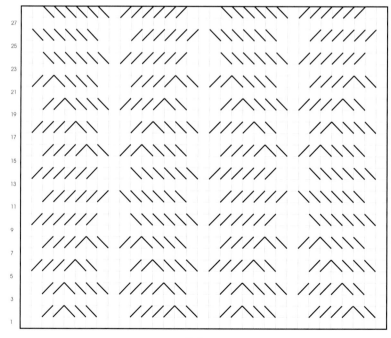

13 sts

= LT   = RT

Row 3: K(0, 3), work across 3rd row of Panels A, D, A, C, A, B, and A, k(0, 3).
Row 4: P(0, 3), work across 4th row of Panels A, B, A, C, A, D, and A, p(0, 3)
These 4 rows set the patt for panels A, B, C, and D.

Panel D

```
                              28
27 ┌─────────────────────┐
                              26
25 │                     │
                              24
23 │                     │
                              22
21 │                     │
                              20
19 │                     │
                              18
17 │                     │
                              16
15 │                     │
                              14
13 │                     │
                              12
11 │                     │
                              10
9  │                     │
                               8
7  │                     │
                               6
5  │                     │
                               4
3  │                     │
                               2
1  └─────────────────────┘
```

13 sts

◁ = FC2   ◁ = BC2

All sizes

Cont in patt until Back measures 15" (17¼", 19¾", 22½", 25¼") [38 (44, 50, 57, 64)cm] from cast-on edge, ending with a wrong-side row.

Shape Back neck

Next row: Patt 31 (33, 35, 37, 39) sts, turn and work on these sts for 1st side of neck.
Dec 1 st at neck edge, on the next 9 rows—22 (24, 26, 28, 30) sts.
Bind off.
With right side facing, slip center 23 (25, 27, 29, 31) sts onto a holder, rejoin yarn to rem sts, patt to end.
Complete to match 1st side.

POCKET LININGS (MAKE 2)

With size 3 needles, cast on 20 (22, 22, 24, 24) sts.

Starting with a p row, work 24 (26, 26, 28, 28) rows in st st.
Leave these sts on a holder.

FRONT

Work as given for Back until 24 (26, 26, 28, 28) rows have been worked in main patt.

Place pockets

Next row: Patt 6 (7, 10, 11, 14), slip next 20 (22, 22, 24, 24) sts on a holder, p across sts of 1st pocket lining, p33, slip next 20 (22, 22, 24, 24) sts on a holder, p across sts of 2nd pocket lining.
Cont in patt across all sts until Front measures 13½" (15¾", 17¾", 20½", 22¾") [34 (40, 45, 52, 58)cm] from cast-on edge, ending with a wrong-side row.

Shape neck

Next row: Patt 36 (38, 40, 42, 44) sts, turn and work on these sts for 1st side of neck.

Dec 1 st at neck edge, on the next 14 rows—22 (24, 26, 28, 30) sts.

Work even until Front measures same as Back to shoulder, ending at side edge.

Bind off.

With right side facing, slip center 13 (15, 17, 19, 21) sts onto a holder, rejoin yarn to rem sts, patt to end.

Complete to match 1st side.

SLEEVES (MAKE 2)

With size 5 needles, cast on 41 (41, 54, 54, 67) sts.

Row 1: K3, *p3, [K1B] 3 times, p3, k4; rep from * ending last rep k3.

Row 2: P3, *k3, [P1B] 3 times, k3, p4; rep from * ending last rep p3.

Row 3: K3, *p2, BC, K1B, FC, p2, k4; rep from * ending last rep k3.

Row 4: P3, *k2, P1B, [k1, P1B] twice, k2, p4; rep from * ending last rep p3.

Row 5: K3, *p1, BC, p1, K1B, p1, FC, p1, k4; rep from * ending last rep k3.

Row 6: P3, *k1, P1B, [k2, p1B] twice, k1, p4; rep from * ending last rep p3.

Row 7: K3, *BC, p2, K1B, p2, FC, k4; rep from * ending last rep k3.

Row 8: P3, *k4, P1B, k4, p4; rep from * ending last rep p3.

Rep these 8 rows once more.

P3 rows, inc 8 (12, 9, 13, 8) sts evenly across last row—49 (53, 63, 67, 75) sts.

Change to size 6 needles and patt.

1–2/3–4 sizes only

Row 1: [K1, p1] 3 (4) times, work across 1st row of Panels D, A and B, [p1, k1] 3 (4) times.

Row 2: [K1, p1] 3 (4) times, work across 2nd row of Panels B, A, and D, [p1, k1] 3 (4) times.

Row 3: [K1, p1] 3 (4) times, work across 3rd row of Panels D, A, and B, [p1, k1] 3 (4) times.

Row 4: [K1, p1] 3 (4) times, work across 2nd row of Panels B, A, and D, [p1, k1] 3 (4) times.

These 4 rows set the patt for Panels D, A, and B with moss st sides.

5–6/7–8/9–10 sizes only

Row 1: [K1, p1] (1, 2, 4) times, work across 1st row of Panels A, D, A, B, and A, [p1, k1] (1, 2, 4) times.

Row 2: [K1, p1] (1, 2, 4) times, work across 2nd row of Panels A, B, A, D, and A, [p1, k1] (1, 2, 4) times.

Row 3: [K1, p1] (1, 2, 4) times, work across 3rd row of Panels A, D, A, B, and A, [p1, k1] (1, 2, 4) times.

Row 4: [K1, p1] (1, 2, 4) times, work across 2nd row of Panels A, B, A, D, and A, [p1, k1] (1, 2, 4) times.

These 4 rows set the patt for Panels A, D, A, B, and A with moss st sides.

All sizes

Cont in patt, *at the same time* inc and work into moss st 1 st at each end of the next and every foll 6th (6th, 10th, 12th, 14th) row until there are 65 (69, 77, 81, 87) sts.

Cont even until Sleeve measures 9¾" (11½", 13", 14½", 16¼") [25 (29, 33, 37, 41)cm] from cast-on edge, ending with a wrong-side row.

Bind off.

NECKBAND

Join right shoulder seam.

With right side facing and size 3 needles, pick up and k20 (19, 22, 21, 24) sts down left front neck, k13 (15, 17, 19, 21) sts from center front holder, pick up and k19 (18, 21, 20, 23) sts up right side of front neck, 9 (8, 9, 8, 9) sts down right side of back neck, k23 (25, 27, 29, 31) sts from back neck holder, 9 (8, 10, 9, 11) sts up left side of back neck—93 (93, 106, 106, 119) sts.

Next row: P3, *k4, P1B, k4, p4; rep from * ending last rep p3.

Starting with Row 1, work 16 rows in welt patt as given for Sleeves.

Bind off loosely in patt.

POCKET TOP

With wrong side facing and size 3 needles, p across sts of pocket top, dec 1 st at center—19 (21, 21, 23, 23) sts.

Work 8 (10, 10, 12, 12) rows in moss st.

Bind off in patt.

FINISHING

Join left shoulder and neckband. Sew on Sleeves. Sew Pocket Lining in place. Join side and sleeve seams.

gwithian blue

The magnificent beach of Gwithian Sands stretches along the north coast of St. Ives Bay, between Hayle Towans to the west and the natural boundary of the cliffs at Godrevy Point to the east. The name *Gwithian* derives from St. Gothian, an Irish missionary who was slain sometime around the fifth or sixth centuries. Gwithian Sands is well known for two reasons: The nearby lighthouse is the setting for Virginia Woolf's novel *To the Lighthouse,* and the shore makes for one of the best surfing beaches in the UK. Our days spent swimming and surfing on this pristine beach have inspired the knitwear in this chapter.

Surfing has been integral to Cornish life since the mid-1960s, and Gwithian Sands attracts a large share of those surfers. Forty years ago, equipment was hard to come by, and a lot of the early surfers in Cornwall resorted to making their own wet suits, cutting them out of neoprene from paper dressmaking patterns and then gluing and taping them together.

Surf's up at Gwithian Sands.

Today, of course, the wet suit is a staple of surfwear, and an important category of clothing all its own. Over the past few years, Gwithian Sands has emerged as a haven for all kinds of water sports, including surfing, kitesurfing, sea-kayaking, and body-boarding. And in 1990, a group of surfers from Gwithian founded Surfers Against Sewage (SAS) with the mission of keeping our seas clean. Gwithian is also a very safe beach for families who want to picnic and swim, with many rock pools for younger children to play in. In my family, we surf and body-board—all with various stages of expertise—and Gwithian is one of our favorite beaches. With just a few cafés on the dunes, the beach remains virtually untouched by commercial developments.

The lighthouse on Godrevy Island, built in 1859, is visible from both Gwithian Sands and St. Ives. Except for the lighthouse and a large population of gulls, Godrevy Island is otherwise deserted, though seals do drop by during certain times of the year. A half-mile-long (.8km) reef extends from the island and has caused many a shipwreck. In 1649, a ship called *Garland*, carrying the possessions of the recently executed Charles I, wrecked here, and some say that you can still find gold buttons on the sands. But it was really Woolf's 1927 novel *To the Lighthouse* that immortalized Godrevy Lighthouse. While her descriptions are recognizably Cornish, Woolf sets the novel on the island of Skye in Scotland. Some speculate she did this as a means of keeping the novel from seeming autobiographical—as she spent her childhood vacations in St. Ives.

> **REFRESHMENTS**

Godrevy Café: Good food with a fantastic view from the first-floor balcony dining area. Located on Godrevy Towans

Sunset Surf Café: Good, simple food with an adjoining surf shop. www.sunsetsurfshop.com

surf hoodie

Sizes

XS (S, M, L, XL, XXL)

Measurements after Washing

Chest: 37¾" (41¾", 45¾", 49½", 53½", 57½") [96 (106, 116, 126, 136, 146)cm]

Length to shoulder: 26" (26½", 26¾", 27", 27½", 28") [66 (67, 68, 69, 70, 71)cm]

Men's sleeve length: 21" (21", 21¼", 21¼", 21¾", 21¾") [53 (53, 54, 54, 55, 55)cm]

Women's sleeve length: 19" (19", 19¼", 19¼", 19¾", 19¾") [48 (48, 49, 49, 50, 50)cm]

Materials

- 10 (10, 11, 11, 12, 12) balls Rowan Denim (100% cotton, 1¾ oz [50g], 108 yd [93m]) in Ecru (A)
- 17½ (17½, 19½, 19½, 21, 21) oz (500 [500, 550, 500 600, 600]g), 1017 (1017, 1094, 1203, 1203) yd (930 [930, 1000, 1100, 1100]m) recycled denim yarn (B)
- Size 5 (3.75mm) needles
- Size 6 (4mm) needles
- Size 6 (4mm) double-pointed needles
- Stitch holder

Gauge

20 sts and 28 rows = 4" (10cm) square in st st using size 6 (4mm) needles before washing.

Abbreviations and Techniques

Refer to pages 18–19.

BACK

With size 5 needles and A, cast on 98 (108, 118, 128, 138, 148) sts.
Beg with a k row, cont in st st.
Work 3 rows.
Change to size 6 needles and work as follows:
Next row (RS): P3, k to last 3 sts, p3.
Next row: K3, p to last 3 sts, k3.
Rep the last 2 rows 10 times more.
Beg with a k row, cont in st st.
Work 4 rows.
Change to B.
Work 26 rows st st.
Change to A.
Work 26 rows st st.
Cont working in stripes of 26 rows alternating between A and B until a total of 118 (120, 122, 124, 126, 128) rows have been worked on size 6 needles.

Shape armholes

Keep continuity of stripe patt.
Bind off 2 sts at beg next 4 (4, 6, 6, 8, 8) rows—90 (100, 106, 116, 122, 132) sts**.
Cont even until 66 (68, 70, 72, 74, 76) rows more have been worked.

Shape Back neck

Next row: K30 (34, 36, 40, 42, 46), turn and work on these sts for 1st side of neck shaping.
Dec 1 st at neck edge on the next 6 rows—24 (28, 30, 34, 36, 40) sts.
Leave sts on holder for shoulder.
With right side facing, slip center 30 (32, 34, 36, 38, 40) sts to holder for back neck.
Rejoin yarn to rem sts, k to end.
Dec 1 st at neck edge on the next 6 rows—24 (28, 30, 34, 36, 40) sts.
Leave sts on holder for shoulder.

FRONT

Work as given for Back to **.
Cont even for 12 rows.

Neck opening

Next row: K42 (47, 50, 55, 58, 63), p3 sts, turn.
Work on these 45 (50, 53, 58, 61, 66) sts only for left side of Front neck.
Next row: K3, p to end.
Keeping 3 rev sts at the neck edge, work 38 (40, 42, 44, 46, 48) more rows.

Shape neck

Next row: K to last 3 sts, place these 3 sts on a holder, turn and work on these sts.
Next row: Bind off 4 sts, p to end.
Next row: K to end.
Next row: Bind off 1 (2, 3, 4, 5, 6) sts, p to end.
Next row: K to end.
Next row: Bind off 3 sts, p to end.
Next row: K to end.

Rep the last 2 rows once more.
Next row: Bind off 2 sts, p to end.
Next row: K to end.
Next row: Bind off 1 st, p to end.
Next row: K to end.
Rep the last 2 rows 4 times more—24 (28, 30, 34, 36, 40) sts.
Leave sts on holder for shoulder.
With right side facing, rejoin yarn to remaining sts, p3, k to end.
Complete right side to match left.

RIGHT SLEEVE
With size 5 needles and A, cast on 48 (52, 56, 60, 64, 68) sts.
Beg with a k row, cont in st st.
Work 3 rows.
Change to size 6 needles and work as follows:
Row 1 (RS): P2, k to last 2 sts, p2.
Row 2: K2, p to last 2 sts, k2.
Rep the last 2 rows once more.
Row 5: P2, m1, k to last 2 sts, m1, p2**.

Row 6: K2, p35 (37, 39, 41, 43, 45), k4, p7 (9, 11, 13, 15, 17), k2.

Thumb opening
Row 7: P2, k7 (9, 11, 13, 15, 17), p2, turn, leave remaining sts on holder.
Work 11 rows on these sts, increasing at side edge (as before, after p2 edging) on 9th and 15th rows, keeping rev st st border of thumb hole correct.
Leave these sts on holder.
With right side facing, rejoin yarn to rem sts, p2, k to last 2 sts, p2.
Work 11 more rows on these sts, increasing at side edge on 9th and 15th rows as before and keeping rev st st border of thumb hole correct.
Row 19 (rejoin pieces): P2, m1, k9 (11, 13, 15, 17, 19), p2 from holder, p2 from needle, k to last 2 sts, p2—56 (60, 64, 68, 72, 76) sts.
Row 20: K2, p to last 2 sts, k2.

Row 21: K to end.
Row 22: P to end.
Work now in striped st st patt (26-row stripes as for Front and Back), inc 1 st 2 sts in from each edge (as before) on Row 25, and every foll 4th row (Rows 29, 33, 37, 41, 45, 49, etc.) until there are 100 (104, 108, 112, 116, 120) sts.

For women's Sleeve only
Cont even until 132 (132, 136, 136, 140, 140) rows have been worked.

For men's Sleeve only
Cont even until 148 (148, 152, 152, 156, 156) rows have been worked.

Shape Sleeve top
Bind off 6 sts at beg of next 2 rows, 3 sts at beg of next 6 rows, 4 sts at beg of next 8 (8, 10, 10, 12, 12) rows. Bind off rem sts.

LEFT SLEEVE
Work as given for right Sleeve to **.
Row 6: K2, p7 (9, 11, 13, 15, 17), k4, p35 (37, 39, 41, 43, 45), k2.

Thumb opening
Row 7: P2, k35 (37, 39, 41, 43, 45), p2, turn, leave remaining sts on holder.
Work 11 rows on these sts, increasing at side edge (as before, after p2 edging) on 9th and 15th rows, keeping rev st st border of thumb hole correct.
Leave these sts on holder.
With right side facing, rejoin yarn to rem sts, p2, k to last 2 sts, p2.
Work 11 more rows on these sts, increasing at side edge on 9th and 15th rows as before and keeping rev st st border of thumb hole correct.
Row 19 (rejoin pieces): P2, m1, k37 (39, 41, 43, 45, 47), p2 from holder, p2 from needle, k to last 2 sts, p2—56 (60, 64, 68, 72, 76) sts.
Row 20: K2, p to last 2 sts, k2.
Complete to match Right Sleeve.

HOOD

Use 3-needle bind-off to join shoulder seams on right side of hoodie.

With size 6 circular needle and A, p across 3 sts from holder for right Front neck, pick up and knit 23 sts up right Front neck, 3 sts down Back neck, k across 30 (32, 34, 36, 38, 40) sts from Back neck holder, 3 sts up Back neck, 23 sts down left Front neck, and p across 3 sts from holder—88 (90, 92, 94, 96, 98) sts.

Working in st st with rev st st border and keeping continuity of 26-row stripes, work 77 (79, 81, 83, 85) rows even (right side facing).

Shape Hood top

Next row: K40 (41, 42, 43, 44, 45), skpo, k4, k2tog, k40 (41, 42, 43, 44, 45).

Work 3 rows even.

Next row: K39 (40, 41, 42, 43, 44), skpo, k4, k2tog, k39 (40, 41, 42, 43, 44).

Work 3 rows even.

Next row: K38 (39, 40, 41, 42, 43), skpo, k4, k2tog, k38 (39, 40, 41, 42, 43).

Work 3 rows even.

Cont in this way dec 2 sts on next and foll 4th row.

Work 1 row.

Split remaining sts so that you have 39 (40, 41, 42, 43, 44) sts on 2 needles.

Graft together with kitchener stitch.

FINISHING

Sew in Sleeves to armholes.

Sew up side and sleeve seams, starting from top of rev st st border on each piece, giving slits at side edges and Sleeve bottoms.

HOOD CORDS (MAKE 2)

With size 5 needles, work 3-st I-cord for 104 rows in 26-row stripe pattern. Attach to point where Hood is picked up from body on the st st part, not on the rev st st border.

fringe bardot top

Inspired by a photograph of the French actress Bridget Bardot, this off-the-shoulder design has been one of Artwork's most successful. Over the years, we have used it in our collections as a handknit, a machine-knit, and a cut-and-sew jersey T-shirt. To create the sun-bleached degradé effect, the fringe has been dipped in a bleach solution (instructions on page 15).

Sizes
XS (S, M, L, XL)

Measurements after Washing
Bust: 33½" (35¾", 38", 40½", 43") [85 (91, 97, 103, 109)cm]
Length to shoulder: 19¼" (19¼", 20", 20", 21") [49 (49, 51, 51, 53)cm]

Materials
▶ 8 (9, 10, 11, 12) balls Elann Den-M-Nit (100% cotton, 1¾ oz [50g], 101 yd [92m]) in Pale Indigo
▶ Size 5 (3.75mm) needles
▶ Size 6 (4mm) needles

Gauge
20 sts and 28 rows = 4" (10cm) square in st st using size 6 needles before washing.

Abbreviations and Techniques
Refer to pages 18–19.

BACK

With size 5 needles, cast on 91 (97, 103, 109, 115) sts.
K11 rows.
Change to size 6 needles and patt.
Row 1 (RS): K to end.
Row 2: P to end.
Row 3: K to end.
Row 4: P to end.
Row 5: P to end.
Row 6: K to end.
Row 7: P to end.
Row 8: K to end.
These 8 rows form the patt and are repeated throughout.
Next row: Patt 4, work 2 tog, patt to last 6 sts, work 2 tog, patt 4.
Work 5 rows.
Rep the last 6 rows 3 times more and the dec row again—81 (87, 93, 99, 105) sts.
Cont even until work measures 4¾" (12cm) from cast-on edge, ending with a wrong-side row.
Change to size 5 needles and work a further 2¼" (6cm) in patt.
Change to size 6 needles.
Work 10 rows.
Inc row: Patt 4, m1, patt to last 4 sts, m1, patt 4.
Work 9 rows.
Rep the last 10 rows once more and the inc row again—87 (93, 99, 105, 111) sts.

Cont in patt until Back measures 14½", (14½", 15, 15, 15¼") [37 (37, 38, 38, 39)cm] from cast-on edge, ending with a wrong-side row.

Shape armholes
Bind off 4 sts at beg of next 2 rows—79 (85, 91, 97, 103) sts.
Dec 1 st at each end of the next and every foll odd row until 71 (75, 79, 83, 87) sts rem.
Cont even until Back measures 21¼" (21¼", 22", 22", 22¾") [54 (54, 56, 56, 58)cm] from cast-on edge, ending with a wrong-side row.

Shape neck
Next row: Patt 10 (11, 12, 13, 14), turn and work on these sts.
Dec 1 st at neck edge on next 4 rows—6 (7, 8, 9, 10) sts.
Work 3 rows even.

Shape shoulders
Bind off.
With right side facing, slip center 51 (53, 55, 57, 59) sts on a holder, patt to end.
Complete to match 1st side.

FRONT
Work as given for Back until Front measures 19" (19", 19¾", 19¾", 20½") [48 (48, 50, 50, 52)cm] from cast-on edge, ending with a wrong-side row.

Shape neck

Next row: Patt 15 (16, 17, 18, 19), turn and work on these sts.

Dec 1 st at neck edge on next 9 rows—6 (7, 8, 9, 10) sts.

Work even until Front matches Back to shoulder shaping, ending at armhole edge.

Shape shoulders

Bind off.

With right side facing, slip center 41 (43, 45, 47, 49) sts on a holder, patt to end.

Complete to match 1st side.

COLLAR

Join right shoulder seam.

With right side facing and size 5 needles, pick up and k24 sts down left side of Front neck, k41 (43, 45, 47, 49) sts from Front neck holder, pick up and k24 sts up right Front neck, 8 sts down right side of Back neck, k51 (53, 55, 57, 59) sts from Back neck holder, pick up and k8 sts up left side of Back neck—156 (160, 164, 168, 172) sts.

Row 1 (RS): K to end.

Row 2: P to end.

Row 3: K to end.

Row 4: P to end.

Rows 5–10: P to end.

These 10 rows form the patt and are repeated throughout.

Cont in patt until collar measures 3" (8cm) from beg.

Change to size 6 needles.

Cont in patt for a further 4" (10cm), ending Row 10.

Bind off.

ARMBANDS

Join left shoulder seam and collar. With size 5 needles and right side facing, pick up and k80 (80, 84, 84, 88) sts evenly around armhole edge.

K 3 rows.

Bind off.

FINISHING

Join side seams.

Fringing

Cut rem yarn into 11" (28cm) lengths and knot 2 strands through every alt st to form fringing.

Dip Bleached

Do without sleeves

Dark Indigo

Bleached ends

gwithian beach bag

This roomy bag is ideal for carrying your towel, swimsuit, and book to the beach. And it is always a great tote for your knitting! Weave stitch is used to create the stripes, and the indigo yarn shown here has been randomly bleached.

BASE

With size 5 double-pointed needles and D, cast on 8 sts.
Taking care not to twist the yarn, join into a ring.
Mark the join.
Round 1: K to end—8 sts.
Round 2: *K1, m1; rep from * to end of round—16 sts.
Round 3: K to end.
Round 4: *K1, m1, k3, m1; rep from * to end of round—24 sts.
Round 5: K to end.
Round 6: *K1, m1, k5, m1; rep from * to end of round—32 sts.
Round 7: K to end.
Round 8: *K1, m1, k7, m1; rep from * to end of round—40 sts.
Round 9: K to end.
Round 10: *K1, m1, k9, m1; rep from * to end of round—48 sts.
Cont working in rounds as set (one round plain knit, one round increase), working stripes for a further 6 rounds in D then 16 rounds each in C, B, and A until a total of 64 rounds have been worked—264 sts.
Change to the circular needle when necessary.
Mark one "corner" of the base as the start of the rounds for the body.

BODY

Work even for 28 rounds in each of D, C, B, and A.

HANDLES

With A, cont as foll:
Round 1: *Yf, sl 1 p-wise, yb, k1; rep from * to end of round.
Round 2: *K1, yf, sl 1 p-wise, yb; rep from * to end of round.
These 2 rounds set the patt.
Rounds 3–4: As Rounds 1 and 2.
Round 5: Patt 22 sts, bind off 22 sts, patt next 109 sts, bind off 22 sts, patt to end of round.
Round 6: Patt 22 sts, cast on 88 sts, patt 110 sts, cast on 88 sts, patt to end of round—396 sts.
Work a further 18 rounds with pattern as set, cast off knitwise. Sew in all ends securely.

FINISHING

Taking a long length of randomly bleached yarn, thread tapestry needle. Beg at 1st round on the body of the bag (D section), weave bleached yarn in and out along row, over 1st st and under the following stitch. On 2nd round, alternate weaving so that yarn goes under 1st stitch and over the next stitch. Repeat on B stripe of bag (omitting sections of C and A), being careful not to pull yarn too tight and keeping tension consistent.

Measurements after Washing
Approximately 40" (102cm) circumference, 31" (79cm) from top of handle to base

Materials
- 4 balls Rowan Denim (100% cotton, 1¾ oz [50g], 108 yd [93m]) in Tennessee (A), 3 balls in Memphis (B), 2 balls in Nashville (C), and 2 balls in Ecru (D)
- Size 5 (3.75mm) double-pointed needles
- Size 5 (3.75mm) circular needle
- Approximately 5⅓ oz (150g), 324 yd (279m) of randomly bleached yarn (instructions on page 12)
- Tapestry needle
- Stitch marker

Gauge
24 sts and 32 rows 4" (10cm) square in st st using size 5 needles before washing.

Abbreviations and Techniques
Refer to pages 18–19.

gwithian beach blanket

This project is an opportunity for you to try out some of the techniques in the "Working with Indigo Yarn" section and to use up some of the gauge swatches you may have produced in creating the other projects for this book. As such, no yarn amounts are provided. Measurements are provided under each individual swatch. There are just a few fillers in moss stitch or stockinette stitch.

Measurements after Washing
Approximately 60" wide x 83" long (150x210cm)

Materials
- Elann Den-M-Nit (100% cotton, 101 yd [92m]) in Pale Indigo (A), Ecru (B), Mid Indigo (C), and Dark Indigo (D)
- Elle True Blue (100% indigo cotton, 118 yd [108m]) in Navy (E) and Bone (F)
- Rowan Denim (100% cotton, 108 yd [93m]) in Nashville (G), Tennessee (H), Ecru (I), and Memphis (J)
- Rowan Handknit Cotton DK (100% cotton, 93 yd [85m]) in Black (K)
- Size 6 (4mm) needles
- Size 5 (3.75mm) needles
- Size 3 (3.25mm) needles

Abbreviations and Techniques
Refer to pages 18–19.

EMBROIDERED CHAIN STITCH (6"x12" (15x30CM))
With A and size 6 needles, cast on 32 sts.
Work 90 rows in st st.
Bind off.

EMBROIDERED CORNWALL (6"x42" (15x105CM))
With B and size 5 needles, cast on 32 sts.
Row 1: *K1, p1; rep from * to end.
Row 2: As Row 1.
Row 3: *P1, k1; rep from * to end.
Row 4: As Row 3.
These 4 rows form the patt (double moss st).
Work a further 310 rows.
Bind off.

ARGYLE-BLEACHED WHITBY CABLE (6"x30" (15x75CM))
With C and size 6 needles, cast on 36 sts.
Follow Panel B from Whitby pattern (page 28), but add an extra 9 sts rev st st each side of cable to make up 36 sts.
Work in patt until 225 rows have been worked.
Bind off.

NEWLYN BACK (6"x38" (15x95CM))
With B and size 5 needles, work the first 6" (15cm) of the Newlyn Jacket pattern (page 32) for the Back.

TIE-BLEACHED STOCKINETTE (6"x36" (15x90CM))
With E and size 6 needles, cast on 35 sts.
Work 254 rows in st st.
Bind off.
Make 2.

PALE MOSS STITCH (6"x30" (15x75CM))
With A and size 5 needles, cast on 32 sts.
Moss st Row 1: *K1, p1; rep from * to end.
Moss st Row 2: P1, k1; rep from * to end.
These 2 rows form the moss st.
Work a further 222 rows.
Bind off.

ECRU WOVEN STITCH (6"x12" (15x30CM))
With B and size 6 needles, cast on 39 sts.
Row 1 (RS): K1, *yf, sl 1 p-wise, yb, k1, rep from * to end.
Row 2: P2, *yb, sl 1 p-wise, yf, p1, rep from * to last st, p1.
These 2 rows form the patt.
Work a further 124 rows.
Bind off.

INDIGO STRIPES (6"x12" (15x30CM))
With G and J and size 6 needles, cast on 32 sts.

Work 92 rows of the foll patt:
Row 1: K to end.
Row 2: P3, k5, p to last 8 sts, k5, p3.
Rep these 2 rows, working in stripes of 4 rows in each color.
Bind off.

CORNISH KNIT (12"x42" (30x105cm))

With G, and size 6 needles, cast on 74 sts.
Work 8 sts in moss st, 1st row of Panel C from the Cornish Knit Frock (page 24), 8 sts moss st, 1st row of Panel A (page 24), 8 sts moss st, 1st row of Panel B (page 24), 8 sts moss st.
Work 316 rows following panels in moss st.
Bind off.

ECRU AND INDIGO STRIPES (12"x12" (30x30cm))

With H and I and size 6 needles, cast on 62 sts.
Work 92 rows patt given for Indigo Stripes swatch (page 58).
Bind off.

ECRU RICE STITCH (6"x30" (15x75cm))

With F and size 5 needles, cast on 37 sts.
Row 1: P1, *k1tbl, p1; rep from * to end.
Row 2: K to end.
These 2 rows form the patt.
Work a further 254 rows.
Bind off.

MID INDIGO STOCKINETTE (6"x30" (15x75cm))

With C and size 6 needles, cast on 32sts.
Work 225 rows st st.
Bind off.

PALE RICE STITCH (6"x18" (15x45cm))

With A and size 6 needles, cast on 32 sts.
Work 114 rows st st.
Bind off.

WEAVE STITCH (8"x8" (20x20cm))

With J and size 6 needles, cast on 40 sts.
Work 60 rows st st.
Bind off.
Use I and H for weaving.

ECRU TREE PATTERN (8"x34" (20x85cm))

With I and size 6 needles, cast on 39 sts.
Row 1 (RS): *K2, p3, K3B, p3, k2, rep from * twice.
Row 2: *P2, k3, P3B, p3, p2, rep from * twice.

Row 3: *K2, p2, BC, K1B, FC, p2, k2, rep from * twice.
Row 4: *P2, k2, (P1B, k1) twice, P1B, k2, p2, rep from * twice.
Row 5: *K2, p1, BC, p1, K1B, p1, FC, p1, k2, rep from * twice.
Row 6: *P2, k1, [P1B, k2] twice, P1B, k1, p2, rep from * twice.
Row 7: *K2, BC, p1, K3B, p1, FC, k2, rep from * twice.
Row 8: *P2, P1B, k2, P3B, k2, P1B, p2, rep from * twice.
These 8 rows form the patt and are repeated throughout.
Work a further 228 rows.
Bind off.

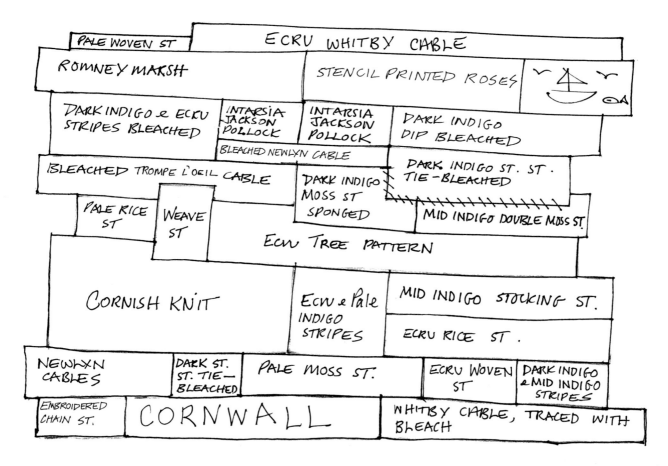

The diagram contains the following handwritten labels:

- PALE WOVEN ST
- ECRU WHITBY CABLE
- ROMNEY MARSH
- STENCIL PRINTED ROSES
- DARK INDIGO & ECRU STRIPES BLEACHED
- INTARSIA JACKSON POLLOCK
- INTARSIA JACKSON POLLOCK
- DARK INDIGO DIP BLEACHED
- BLEACHED NEWLYN CABLE
- BLEACHED TROMPE L'OEIL CABLE
- DARK INDIGO MOSS ST SPONGED
- DARK INDIGO ST. ST. TIE-BLEACHED
- PALE RICE ST
- WEAVE ST
- MID INDIGO DOUBLE MOSS ST.
- ECRU TREE PATTERN
- CORNISH KNIT
- ECRU & PALE INDIGO STRIPES
- MID INDIGO STOCKING ST.
- ECRU RICE ST.
- NEWLYN CABLES
- DARK ST. ST. TIE-BLEACHED
- PALE MOSS ST.
- ECRU WOVEN ST
- DARK INDIGO & MID INDIGO STRIPES
- EMBROIDERED CHAIN ST.
- CORNWALL
- WHITBY CABLE, TRACED WITH BLEACH

BLEACHED TROMPE L'OEIL CABLE (9"x24" (22.5x60CM))

With D and size 6 needles, cast on 35 sts.
Work 306 rows st st.
Bind off.

SPONGE-BLEACHED MOSS STITCH (6"x26" (15x65CM))

With G and size 3 needles, cast on 32 sts.
Moss st Row 1: *K1, p1; rep from * to end.
Moss st Row 2: *P1, k1; rep from * to end.
These 2 rows form the moss st.
Work a further 178 rows.
Bind off.

DOUBLE MOSS STITCH (6"x30" (15x75CM))

With C and size 3 needles, cast on 32 sts.
Row 1: *K1, p1; rep from * to end.
Row 2: As Row 1.
Row 3: *P1, k1; rep from * to end.
Row 4: As Row 3.
These 4 rows form the double moss st.
Work a further 221 rows double moss st.

BOTTLE-BLEACHED INDIGO AND ECRU STRIPES (12"x24" (30x60CM))

With G and I and size 6 needles, cast on 47 sts.
Work 180 rows in patt given for Indigo Stripes swatch (page 58).
Bind off.

BLEACHED NEWLYN CABLE (6"x26" (15x65CM))

With C and size 6 needles, cast on 30 sts.
Row 1: P8, CR14, p8.
Row 2: K8, p14, k8.
Row 3: P7, CR5B, k6, CR5F, p7.
Row 4: K7, p4, k1, p6, k1, p4, k7.
Row 5: P6, CR5B, p1, k6, p1, CR5F, p6.
Row 6: K6, p4, k2, p6, k2, p4, k6.
Row 7: P5, CR5B, p2, C6B, p2, CR5F, p5.
Row 8: K5, p4, k3, p6, k3, p4, k5.
Row 9: P4, CR5B, p3, k6, p3, CR5F, p4.
Row 10: K4, p4, k4, p6, k4, p4, k4.
Row 11: P3, CR5B, p4, k6, p4, CR5F, p3.
Row 12: K3, p4, k5, p6, k5, p4, k3.
Row 13: P2, CR5B, p5, C6B, p5, CR5F, p2.
Row 14: K2, p4, k6, p6, k6, p4, k2.
Row 15: P2, k4, p6, k6, p6, k4, p2.
Row 16: As Row 14.
Row 17: As Row 15.
Row 18: As Row 14.
Row 19: P2, CR5F, p5, C6B, p5, CR5B, p2.
Row 20: K3, p4, k5, p6, k5, p4, k3.
Row 21: P3, CR5F, p4, k6, p4, CR5B, p3.

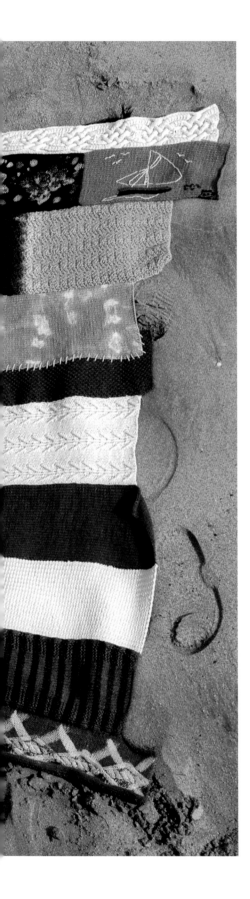

Row 22: K4, p4, k4, p6, k4, p4, k4.
Row 23: P4, CR5F, p3, k6, p3, CR5B, p4.
Row 24: K5, p4, k3, p6, k3, p4, k5.
Row 25: P5, CR5F, p2, C6B, p2, CR5B, p5.
Row 26: K6, p4, k2, p6, k2, p4, k6.
Row 27: P6, CR5F, p1, k6, p1, CR5B, p6.
Row 28: K7, p4, k1, p6, k1, p4, k7.
Row 29: P7, CR5F, k6, CR5B, p7.
Row 30: K8, p14, k8.
Work a further 150 rows.

JACKSON POLLOCK ON INTARSIA 1 (12"x6" (30x15CM))

With G size and size 6 needles, cast on 60 sts.
Work 10 rows st st.

Begin intarsia square:
Row 1: K20 G, 20 K, 20 G.
Row 2: P20 G, 20 K, 20 G.
Rep the last 2 rows 14 times more.
Using G work 10 rows st st.
Bind off.

JACKSON POLLOCK ON INTARSIA 2 (9"x36" (22.5x90CM))

Work as above using J instead of G.

Begin intarsia square:
Row 1: *P3, BC, K1B, FC, p2, rep from * to end.
Row 2: K3, [P1B, K1] twice, P1B, k2.
Row 3: P2, BC, p1, K1B, p1, FC, p1.
Row 4: [K2, P1B] 3 times, k1.
Row 5: P1, BC, p1, K3B, p1, FC.
Row 6: K1, P1B, k2, P3B, k2, P1B.
Rep these 6 rows 44 times more—270 rows total.
Bind off.

ROMNEY MARSH DIAMONDS (6"x36" (15x90CM))

With C and size 6 needles, cast on 33 sts.
Working from Panel C from the Romney Marsh Smock (page 38),

work 280 rows patt.
Bind off.

STOCKINETTE WITH STENCILED ROSES (6"x36" (15x90CM))

With E and size 6 needles, cast on 35 sts.
Work 306 rows st st.
Bind off.

DOUBLE MOSS STITCH WITH EMBROIDERED BOAT (6"x12" (15x30CM))

With H and size 5 needles, cast on 32 sts.
Row 1: *K1, p1; rep from * to end.
Row 2: As Row 1.
Row 3: *P1, k1; rep from * to end.
Row 4: As Row 3.
These 4 rows form the double moss st.
Work a further 88 rows double moss st.
Bind off.

PALE WOVEN STITCH (3"x25" (7.5x65CM))

With A and size 6 needles, cast on 19 sts.
Row 1 (RS): K1 *yf, sl 1 p-wise, yb, k1, rep from * to end.
Row 2: P2, *yb, sl 1 p-wise, yf, p1, rep from * to last st, p1.
These 2 rows form the patt.
Work a further 188 rows.
Bind off.

ECRU WHITBY CABLE (3"x65" (7.5x165CM))

With I and size 6 needles, cast on 23 sts.
Work Panel C from Whitby Sweater (page 28) for a total of 18 patt repeats.

FINISHING

Sew all pieces together as shown in illustration and photographs. Weave in all ends on the back of the work.

beaded mp3 player pouch

Created in one solid color with glass beads knitted in, the Beaded MP3 Player Pouch is the perfect way to protect your MP3 player in style. To make the striped version, shown right, visit the Artwork website, www.artworkbygottelier.co.uk, for the full pattern.

Materials

► 1 ball Elann Den-M-Nit (100% cotton, 1¾ oz [50g], 101 yd [92m]) in Mid Indigo
► 52 size 5/0 glass embroidery beads in each of 4 colors— white, turquoise, silver, and dark blue
► Size 5 (3.75mm) double-pointed needles
► Size E/4 (3.5mm) crochet hook

Measurements after Washing
To fit a standard-size MP3 player

Gauge
21 sts and 29 rows = approximately 4" (10cm) in circular st st.

Abbreviations and Techniques
Refer to pages 18–19.

POUCH

Thread beads onto yarn, starting with 17 white, 17 turquoise, 17 silver, and 17 dark blue. Repeat this sequence twice more.

With size 5 needles, cast on 34 sts. Join into a round.

Round 1: K to end.

Round 2: *K1, bead 1, rep from * to end of round.

Repeat these 2 rounds until the beads are used up, and then cont in st st until work measures 4¼" (11cm), or the depth of your MP3 player.

Next round: P2, k10, p22.

Next round: K14, bind off 20 p-wise.

Cont in rows on rem 14 sts.

Row 1: K2, p10, k2.

Row 2: K to end.

Rep the last 2 rows for 2" (5cm), ending with a 1st row.

Next row: K2, skpo, k to last 4 sts, k2tog, k2.

Next row: K2, p8, k2.

Buttonhole row: K2, skpo, k1, k2tog, yf, k1, k2tog, k2.

Next row: K to end.

Bind off rem sts p-wise.

FINISHING

Sew up bottom. With size E/4 hook, make a chain to length required, work 1 sc into each chain, or knit an I-cord to length required.

Make a button by sewing through 4 beads to make one big bead.

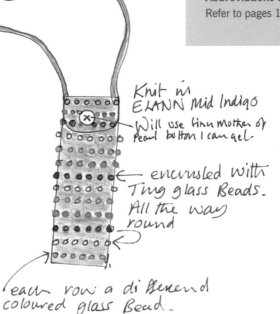

Knit in ELANN Mid Indigo
Will use linn mother of Pearl button I can gel.

encrusted with Tiny glass Beads. All the way round

each row a different coloured glass Bead.

50°02' NORTH, 5°37' WEST

lamorna blue

The tiny village of Lamorna lies along a wooded valley leading down to a small harbor that is wedged between huge granite cliffs. To the east lies Mousehole and to the west, St. Loy's Cove.

Lamorna has held great fascination for our family ever since our young boys used to hold cork-boat races in the valley's stream. Every spring, as we take our walks along that rushing stream, which cascades into the harbor, we marvel at the wood anemones and bluebells that carpet the valley. No wonder so many artists have settled here!

The village of Lamorna originally began as an artists' colony in the early nineteenth century, when Lamorna Birch, a charismatic painter who had already settled in the valley, introduced several of the Newlyn artists to its tranquil, unspoiled scenery. In fact, Lamorna became so popular among these artists that the locals, primarily fishing families and farmers, began to complain that the new settlers were making the area surburban.

The Lamorna Stream. An artist's studio lies beyond the trees.

> REFRESHMENTS

Cove Cottage Tea Gardens: One of the best cream tea spots in all Cornwall! Set in a subtropical garden that leads down to the sea. Located at St. Loy's Cove, which is only reachable on foot. For guided walks, visit www.adventureline.co.uk.

The Cove Restaurant and Terrace Bar: Spectacular view of Lamorna Cove. www.thecovecornwall.co.uk

Lamorna Cove Café: Fantastic selection of cakes and homemade desserts.

The Lamorna Wink: Traditional pub with nautical memorabilia on the walls and ceiling.

> GARDENS

Chygurno Gardens: Dramatic gardens carved into the cliff with an exotic mix of plants from around the world.

Trewoofe Gardens: Millstream gardens that once belonged to artists Ella and Charles Naper. www.lamorna-valley.co.uk

Lamorna is known for its lovely gardens.

Catching forty winks near the Lamorna Wink, a pub in the Lamorna valley.

Although Birch founded the art movement in the village, the two local artists who really fascinate Patrick and me are Ella and Charles Naper, a married couple who arrived in the valley around the beginning of the twentieth century. The two came to Cornwall in search of an unconventional, more bohemian way of life. According to James Branfield, author of the history *Ella and Charles Naper: Art and Life at Lamorna*, the move reflected the Napers' decision "to care only about what really mattered to them, the enjoyment of nature, the nurturing of friendships, and the creation of beautiful things: a home and a garden, jewelery, ceramics, and painting." In fact, artists today still come to Lamorna to live the dream shared by Ella and Charles Naper.

By all accounts, Lamorna has hardly changed since the Napers' day. The narrow road through the valley is now tarmac, but the woods and wildflowers are abundant and beautiful. The Lamorna Wink, a pub lying halfway along the valley path, is still there, with its wonderful selection of nautical memorabilia plastered all over the walls and ceiling. And you can see many of the cottages and artists' studios that were set up during the colony's heyday. The Welsh poet Dylan Thomas was a frequent visitor to one of cottages, called Oriental Cottage, where the artist John Armstrong lived. According to local lore, a thornbush just outside the cottage was named for Thomas, who frequently fell into it on his return from a session at the Wink.

In this chapter, we try to conjure up the idyllic life we imagine the Napers must have led in the Lamorna Valley, based on old photographs and paintings from the time. The knitwear we've designed for this chapter is a modern interpretation of the bohemian clothes these artists wore.

artist's waistcoat

Gentlemen artists of the Victorian era would paint in very formal attire, often sporting three-piece suits in the heat of the day! This design is based on the fitted waistcoats popular during that time. Its embroidered back, which is created using the Swiss darning technique, mimics the woven pinstripe fabric that likely would have been used to create the original garments.

Sizes
S (M, L)

Measurements after Washing
Chest: 32 (34²⁄₃", 37") [82 (88, 94)cm]
Length to shoulder: 18" (19", 19¾") [46 (48, 50)cm]

Materials
▸ 6 (7, 8) balls Elann Den-M-Nit (100% cotton, 1¾ oz [50g], 101 yd [92m]) in Mid Indigo and 1 ball in Ecru for chain stitch embroidery
▸ Size 3 (3.25mm) needles
▸ Size 6 (4mm) needles
▸ Stitch holder
▸ Sewing needle and thread
▸ 4 buttons, ⅝" (1.5cm) in diameter

Gauge
20 sts and 28 rows = 4" (10cm) square in st st using size 6 needles before washing.

Abbreviations and Techniques
Refer to pages 18–19.

BACK
With size 3 needles, cast on 86 (92, 98) sts.
Moss st Row 1: *K1, p1; rep from * to end.
Moss st Row 2: *P1, k1; rep from * to end.
Rep these 2 rows once more.
Change to size 6 needles.
Beg with a k row, cont in st st.
Work 6 (8, 10) rows.
Dec row: K26, skpo, k to last 28 sts, k2tog, k26.
Work 9 rows.
Rep the last 10 rows twice more and the dec row again.
Work 11 rows.
Inc row: K26, m1, k to last 26 sts, m1, k26.
Work 13 rows in st st
Inc row: K26, m1, k to last 26 sts, m1, k26—82 (88, 94) sts.
Work 11 rows in st st.

Shape armholes
Bind off 4 sts at beg of next 2 rows.
Bind off 3 (4, 5) sts at beg of next 2 rows—68 (72, 76) sts.
Dec 1 st at each end of following 4 rows.
P 1 row.
Dec 1 st at each end of following 2 rows.
Dec 1 st at each end of following 2 right-side rows.

Dec 1 st at each end of next row.
Dec 1 st at each end of following 3rd row 4 times.
Work 5 rows even, then dec 1 st at each end of next row—40 (44, 48) sts.
Work 39 rows even.

Shape shoulders
Next row: K8 (9, 10) sts, w&t.
Next row: P8 (9, 10).
Next row: K5 (6, 7) sts, w&t.
Next row: P5 (6, 7).
Next row: Bind off 32 (35, 38) sts, knitting wraps along with sts when casting off, k8 (9, 10).
Next row: P5 (6, 7), w&t.
Next row: K5 (6, 7).
Next row: Bind off p-wise, purling wrap along with st when binding off.

POCKET LININGS

Lower pocket (make 2)
With size 6 needles, cast on 14 sts.
Work 20 rows moss st, leaving sts on a holder.

Breast pocket
With size 6 needles, cast on 7 sts.
Work 18 rows moss st, leaving sts on a holder.

LEFT FRONT
With size 3 needles, cast on 46 (49, 52) sts.

Moss st Row 1: K0 (1, 0), *p1, k1; rep from * to end.
Moss st Row 2: *K1, p1; rep from * to last 0 (1, 0) sts, k0 (1, 0).
Rep these 2 rows once more.
Change to size 6 needles.
Cont in st st and moss st stripe pattern:
Next row: K11 (12, 13), moss st 11 (as set), k11 (12, 13), moss st to end.
Next row: Moss st 13 (14, 15), p11 (12, 13), moss st 11, p11 (12, 13).
Rep the last 2 rows 2 (3, 4) times more.
Dec row: Patt 25 (26, 27) sts, skpo, patt to end.
Patt 9 rows.
Rep the last 10 rows once more.

Place pocket

Next row (dec row): Patt 11 (12, 13) sts, slip the next 14 sts onto a holder, patt across 14 sts from one pocket lining, skpo, patt to end.
Patt 9 rows.
Dec row: Patt 25 (26, 27) sts, skpo, patt to end.
Patt 11 rows.
Inc row: Patt 25 (26, 27), m1, patt to end.
Patt 13 rows.
Inc row: Patt 25 (26, 27), m1, patt to end—44 (47, 50) sts.

Shape neck

Next row: Patt 3 sts, place on a holder for collar, work 2 tog, patt to end.
Dec 1 st at neck edge on next and 3 foll alt rows.

Work 3 rows even.
Next row: Bind off 4 sts, patt to end.
Patt 1 row.
Next row: Bind off 3 (4, 5) sts, patt to last 2 sts, work 2 tog.
Work 3 rows keeping neck edge even while dec 1 st at armhole on every row, then on next row dec 1 st each end.
Work 1 row even.
Dec 1 st at armhole edge only on next 2 rows, then 1 st at neck edge only on foll row.
Dec 1 st at armhole on next and foll alt row, ending with right side facing.

Place breast pocket

Next row: Work 2 tog, patt 4, slip next 7 sts to holder for pocket top, patt across 7 sts from breast pocket lining, patt to end.

Work 1 row even.
Dec 1 st at neck on next row, then 1 st at armhole on next and foll 3rd row.
Work 1 row even.
Dec 1 st at neck on next row, 1 st at armhole on next and foll 3rd row.
Work 1 row even.
Dec 1 st at neck edge on next row, then work 3 rows even.
Dec one st at armhole edge on next row.
Dec at neck only on next row, then every foll 3rd row until 5 (6, 7) sts rem.
Work 19 rows even to match Back.
Bind off.

RIGHT FRONT

With size 3 needles, cast on 46 (49, 52) sts.
Moss st Row 1: K0 (1, 0), *p1, k1; rep from * to end.

Moss st Row 2: *K1, p1; rep from * to last 0 (1, 0) sts, k0 (1, 0).

Rep these 2 rows once more.

Change to size 6 needles.

Cont in st st and moss st stripe pattern.

Next row: Moss st 13 (14, 15), k11 (12, 13), moss st 11, k11 (12, 13).

Next row: P11 (12, 13), moss st 11, p11 (12, 13), moss st to end.

Rep the last 2 rows 2 (3, 4) times more.

Dec row: Patt to last 27 (28, 29), k2tog, patt to end.

Patt 9 rows.

Rep the last 10 rows once more.

Place pocket

Patt 2, yf, k2tog, patt 13 (14, 15) sts, k2tog, slip the next 14 sts onto a holder, patt across 14 sts from one pocket lining, patt to end.

Patt 9 rows.

Dec row: Patt 2, yf, k2tog, patt to last 27 (28, 29), k2tog, patt to end.

Patt 9 rows.

Buttonhole row: Patt 2, yf, k2tog, patt to end.

Patt 1 row.

Inc row: Patt to last 25 (26, 27), m1, patt to end.

Patt 7 rows.

Buttonhole row: Patt 2, yf, k2tog, patt to end.

Patt 5 rows.

Shape neck

Inc row: Patt 3, slip these sts onto a holder for front band, work 2 tog, patt to last 25 (26, 27), m1, patt to end.

Complete to match left Front, reversing all shapings and omitting breast pocket.

POCKET TOPS

Lower pockets (make 2)

With size 3 needles, work across 14 sts on holder in moss st.

Moss st 3 rows.

Bind off in patt.

Breast pocket (make 1)

With size 3 needles, work across 7 sts on holder in moss st.

Moss st 3 rows.

Bind off in patt.

ARMBANDS

Join shoulder seams.

With size 3 needles, pick up and k103 (107, 111) sts around each armhole.

Work 4 rows moss st.

Bind off in patt.

COLLAR

With size 3 needles, slip 3 sts onto needle from holder on right Front, join yarn, pick up and k 55 (57, 59) sts up right Front neck, 33 (35, 37) sts across Back neck, 55 (57, 59) down left Front neck, and patt across 3 sts from right front neck holder—149 (155, 161) sts.

Patt 1 row.

Next row: Patt 91 (95, 99), w&t.

Next row: Patt 36 (38, 40), w&t

Next row: Patt 39 (41, 44), w&t.

Work all wraps with the wrapped st from now on.

Next row: Patt 42 (44, 47), w&t.

Cont this way, working 3 sts more on each row until all collar sts have been worked. Work 1 more complete row.

Bind off loosely in patt.

FINISHING

Using either mattress st or back st, join side and armband seams. Sew in all ends neatly. Sew on buttons to correspond to buttonholes. Wash and dry garment before chain stitching pinstripe lines onto Back with the Ecru yarn, spacing garter stripes evenly 6 sts apart, or as desired. Chain stitching on garment as shown lies in the middle of stitches, not between stitches. Stitch Pocket Linings and Pocket Tops in place.

artist's smock

Traditional artists' smocks of the nineteenth century were woven in canvas or calico and helped artists to protect their clothes. The Artwork version offers a sophisticated update.

BACK

With size 3 needles, cast on 112 (120, 128, 138, 148, 160) sts.
Row 1: *K1, p1; rep from * to end.
Row 2: *P1, k1; rep from * to end.
Rep the last 2 rows 3 times more.
Change to size 6 needles.
Beg with a k row, cont in st st.
Work 12 (14, 16, 18, 20, 22) rows even.
Row 13: K29 (31, 33, 35, 37, 39), skpo, k to last 31 (33, 35, 37, 39, 41) sts, k2tog, k29 (31, 33, 35, 37, 39).
Work 11 rows even.
Row 25: K29 (31, 33, 35, 37, 39), skpo, k to last 31 (33, 35, 37, 39, 41) sts, k2tog, k29 (31, 33, 35, 37, 39).
Work 9 rows even.
Rep the last 10 rows 8 times more and the dec row again—92 (100, 108, 118, 128, 140) sts.
Work 9 rows even.

Shape armhole

Dec 1 st at each end of the next and 4 foll alt rows—82 (90, 98, 108, 118, 130) sts.
Work 16 (18, 22, 24, 28, 32) rows.
Cont in smock pattern.
Patt Row 1: P24 (28, 28, 33, 34, 40), k2, [p2, k2] 8 (8, 10, 10, 12, 12) times, p24 (28, 28, 33, 34, 40).
Patt Row 2: K24 (28, 28, 33, 34, 40), p2 [k2,p2] 8 (8, 10, 10, 12, 12) times, k24 (28, 28, 33, 34, 40).
Patt Row 3: As Row 1.
Patt Row 4: K24 (28, 28, 33, 34, 40), p2, *insert right-hand needle from front between 6th and 7th sts on left-hand needle and draw through a loop, slip this loop onto left-hand needle and k it together with the 1st st on left-hand needle; k1, p2, k2, p2*, rep from * to * 3 (3, 4, 4, 5, 5) times more, k24 (28, 28, 33, 34, 40).
Rows 5 and 7: As Row 1.
Row 6: As Row 2.
Row 8: K24 (28, 28, 33, 34, 40), p2, k2, p2, *insert right-hand needle from front between 6th and 7th sts on left-hand needle and draw through a loop, slip this loop to left-hand needle and knit it together with the 1st st on left-hand needle; k1, p2, k2, p2*, rep from * to * 2 (2, 3, 3, 4, 4) times more, k2, p2, k24 (28, 28, 33, 34, 40).
These 8 rows form the patt.
Work an additional 40 rows.

Shape shoulder and Back neck

Next row: Bind off 7 (8, 9, 10, 11, 12) sts at beg of next row, k until there are 19 (21, 23, 25, 28, 30) sts on right-hand needle, turn, and work on these sts for 1st side of Back neck.
Next row: Bind off 1 st, p to end.
Next row: Bind off 7 (8, 9, 10, 11, 12) sts, work to last 2 sts, k2tog.
Next row: Bind off 1 st, p to end.
Bind off rem 9 (10, 11, 12, 14, 15) sts.
Rejoin yarn to rem sts, bind off center 30 (32, 34, 38, 40, 42) sts, patt to end.
Complete to match 1st side of neck shaping.

FRONT

With size 3 needles, cast on 102 (110, 118, 128, 138, 150) sts.
Row 1: *K1, p1; rep from * to end.

Sizes
XS (S, M, L, XL, XXL)

Measurements after Washing
Bust: 36 (39½", 42½", 46½", 50¼", 55") [91 (100, 108, 118, 128, 140)cm]
Length to shoulder: 26 (26½", 26½", 27¼", 28¼", 29¼") [66 (67, 69, 70, 72, 74)cm]
Sleeve length: 19" (19, 19¼", 19¼", 19¾", 19¾") [48 (48, 49, 49, 50, 50)cm]

Materials
- 17 (18, 19, 21, 22, 24) balls Elann Den-M-Nit (100% cotton, 1¾ oz [50g], 101 yd [92m]) in Ecru
- Size 3 (3.25mm) needles
- Size 6 (4mm) needle
- Size 3 (3.25mm) circular needle
- 2 large buttons
- 2 small buttons
- Sewing needle and thread

Gauge
20 sts and 28 rows = 4" (10cm) square in st st using size 6 needles before washing.

Abbreviations and Techniques
Refer to pages 18–19.

Row 2: *P1, k1; rep from * to end.
Rep the last 2 rows 3 times more.
Change to size 6 needles.
Beg with a k row, cont in st st.
Work 12 (14, 16, 18, 20, 22) rows even.
Row 13: K29 (31, 33, 35, 37, 39),
skpo, k to last 31 (33, 35, 37, 39, 41)
sts k2tog, k29 (31, 33, 35, 37, 39).
Work 11 rows even.
 Row 25: K29 (31, 33, 35, 37, 39),
skpo, k to last 31 (33, 35, 37, 39, 41)
sts k2tog, k29 (31, 33, 35, 37, 39).
Work 9 rows even.
Rep the last 10 rows 8 times more
and the dec row again—82 (90, 98,
108, 118, 130) sts.
Work 5 rows even.

Front opening
Next row: K41 (45, 49, 54, 59, 65),
turn, and work on these sts for 1st
side of neck. Leave rem 41 (45, 49, 54,
59, 65) sts on a holder for right Front.
Work 3 rows even.

Shape armhole
Dec 1 st at beg of next and 4 foll alt
rows—36 (40, 44, 49, 54, 60) sts.
Work even for a further 38 (40, 42,
44, 46, 48) rows.

Shape neck
Bind off 2 (3, 4, 4, 5, 8) sts at beg of
next row and 2 sts at beg of foll 5 (5,
5, 6, 6, 6) alt rows, and 1 st on next
alt row—23 (26, 29, 32, 36, 39) sts.
Work even until Front matches Back
to shoulder shaping, ending at
armhole edge.

Shape shoulders
Bind off 7 (8, 9, 10, 11, 12) sts at beg
of next and foll alternate row.
Bind off rem 9 (10, 11, 12, 14, 15) sts.
With right side facing, rejoin yarn to
rem sts, work to end.
Complete to match 1st side, reversing
all shapings.

LEFT SLEEVE
With size 3 needles, cast on 44 (48,
52, 56, 60, 64) sts.

Row 1: *K1, p1; rep from * to end.
Row 2: *P1, k1; rep from * to end.
Rep the last 2 rows once more.
Buttonhole Row 1: K1, p1, bind off
2 sts, patt to end.
Buttonhole Row 2: Patt to end,
casting on 2 sts over those bound
off in previous row.
Work 2 more rows.
Change to size 6 needles.
Row 1 (inc row): Moss st 3, k1 (3,
5, 2, 4, 6), [m1, k5 (5, 5, 6, 6, 6] 5
times, m1, k1, p1, k4, m1, k5 (6, 7,
8, 9, 10), m1, k1 (2, 3, 4, 5, 6), moss
st 3—52 (56, 60, 64, 68, 72) sts.
Row 2: Moss st 3, p12 (14, 16, 18,
20, 22), k1, p33 (35, 37, 39, 41, 43),
moss st 3.
Note: The purl st showing on the
right side is the fake sleeve seam.
You will increase each side of this st
the way you would at the side edges
of sleeves.
Work 2 rows even, keeping
continuity of 3 sts moss st at edges
and purl st "seam."
Row 5 (RS): Moss st 3, k32 (34, 36,
38, 40, 42), m1, k1, p1, k1, m1, k11
(13, 15, 17, 19, 21), moss st 3—54
(58, 62, 66, 70, 74) sts.
Row 6: Moss st 3, p13 (15, 17, 19,
21, 23), k1, p34 (36, 38, 40, 42, 44),
moss st 3.
Work 2 rows even.
Row 9: Moss st 3, k33 (35, 37, 39,
41, 43), m1, k1, p1, k1, m1, k12
(14, 16, 18, 20, 22), moss st 3—56
(60, 64, 68, 72, 76) sts.
Work 3 rows even.
Row 13: Moss st 3, k34 (36, 38, 40,
42, 44), m1, k1, p1, k1, m1, k13
(15, 17, 19, 21, 23), moss st 3—58
(62, 66, 70, 74, 78) sts.
Work 7 rows even.
Row 21: Inc as set either side of
"seam" line—60 (64, 68, 72, 76,
80) sts.
Work 2 rows even.
Beg working in rounds.
Next round: Slip 1st 57 (61, 65, 69,
73, 77) sts onto circular needle. Slip

last 3 sts (moss sts) onto a
spare needle and place behind the
first 3 sts on the circular needle
(the moss sts).
Next round: [Knit next st on
circular needle tog with next st on
spare needle] 3 times, work to end
of round—57 (61, 65, 69, 73, 77) sts.
Cont in rounds of knit sts, keeping
the "fake seam" a purl st.
Work 1 (1, 3, 3, 5, 5) rounds even.
Next round: Inc either side of
"seam" as set.
Work 7 rounds even.
Next round: Inc as set.
Work 3 rounds even.
Next round: Inc as set.
Rep the last 12 rounds until there
are 93 (97, 101, 105, 107, 113) sts.
Work 3 rounds even.
Next round: Inc as set.
Work 4 (4, 4, 4, 6, 6) rounds even,
ending last round 27 (29, 31, 33, 35,
37) sts *after* purl st of fake seam.
Beg smocking pattern.
Round 1: P2 [k2, p2] 10 times, work
to end of round.
Rounds 2 and 3: As Round 1.
Round 4: P2, *insert right-hand
needle from Front between 6th and
7th sts on left-hand needle and draw
through a loop, slip this loop onto
left-hand needle and knit it together
with the 1st st on left-hand needle;
k1, p2, k2, p2*, rep from * to * 4
times more, work to end.
Round 5: As Round 1, but ending
at the last knit st before the "fake
seam" (the purl st is the first st on
left-hand needle).
Now work in rows by working
backwards and forwards on the
circular needle.
Next row: Bind off 2 sts, patt to end.

Shape sleeve top
Keeping smocking pattern correct,
dec 1 st at beg of foll 9 rows—84
(88, 92, 96, 100, 104) sts.
Bind off 2 sts at beg of next 16 (18,
20, 22, 24, 26) rows—52 sts.

Bind off 3 sts at beg next 6 rows, 4 sts at beg of foll 4 rows.
Bind off rem 18 sts.

RIGHT SLEEVE

With size 3 needles, cast on 44 (48, 52, 56, 60, 64) sts.
Row 1: *K1, p1; rep from * to end.
Row 2: *P1, k1; rep from * to end.
Rep the last 2 rows once more.
Buttonhole Row 1: Patt to last 4 sts, bind off 2 sts, p1.
Buttonhole Row 2: Patt to end, casting on 2 sts over those bind off in previous row.
Work 2 more rows.
Change to size 6 needles.
Row 1 (inc row): Moss st 3, k1 (2, 3, 4, 5, 6), m1, k5 (6, 7, 8, 9, 10), m1, k4, p1, k1, m1 [k5 (5, 5, 6, 6, 6) sts), m1] 5 times, k1 (3, 5, 2, 4, 6), moss st 3—52 (56, 60, 64, 68, 72) sts.
Row 2: Moss st 3, p33 (35, 37, 39, 41, 43), k1, p12 (14, 16, 18, 20, 22), moss st 3.
Cont now working increases either side of fake seam as for Left Sleeve until 23 rows have been worked.
Beg working in rounds.
Next round: Slip first 3 sts (moss sts) onto a spare needle, slip rem 57 (61, 65, 69, 73, 77) sts onto a small circular needle, place the first 3 sts behind the sts on the circular needle.
Next round: Work to last 3 sts on circular needle, [knit next st on circular needle tog with next st on spare needle] 3 times—57 (61, 65, 69, 73, 77) sts.
Cont now as for Left Sleeve.

FRONT EDGING

With size 3 circular needle, pick up and k35 (36, 37, 38, 39, 40) sts down left side of neck opening and 35 (36, 37, 38, 39, 40) up right side of neck opening.
Work 2-st I-cord border all along these 70 (72, 74, 76, 78, 80, 82) sts.

COLLAR

Join shoulder seams.
Beg at right Front neck and with size 3 circular needle, pick up and knit 33 (35, 37, 39, 41, 43) sts across top of I-cord border and up Front neck, 5 sts down right Back neck, 31 (33, 35, 37, 39, 41) across Back neck, 5 sts up left Back neck and 33 (35, 37, 39, 41, 43) sts down left Front neck—107 (113, 119, 125, 131, 137) sts.
Work in moss st for 10 (10, 12, 12, 14, 14) rows, then inc 1 st at each end of next and 3 foll 8 rows—115 (121, 127, 133, 139, 145) sts.
Next row: Patt 17, bind off next 81 (87, 93, 99, 105, 111) sts, patt to end—17 sts left at each end of collar.

Shape collar tip
Next row: Patt 17, turn.
Next row: Patt 16, w&t.
Next row: Patt to end.
Next row: Patt 14, w&t.
Next row: Patt 12, w&t.
Next row: Patt 11, w&t.
Next row: Patt 10, w&t.
Next row: Patt 9, w&t.
Next row: Patt 7, w&t.
Next row: Patt 5, w&t.
Next row: Patt 3, w&t.
Next row: Work to end of row, working all sts, including any wraps.
Bind off.
Rejoin yarn to inner edge of collar and work 2nd tip to match 1st.
With RS of collar facing and size 6 needles, pick up and k177 (188, 199, 210, 221, 232) sts evenly around entire collar edge, bind off. This helps stabilize and neaten the collar edge around the shaping.

POCKETS (MAKE 2)

With size 6 needles, cast on 32 (34, 36, 38, 40, 42) sts.

Beg with a k row, work 50 (50, 52, 52, 54, 54) rows in st st.
Change to size 3 needles.
Work 5 rows in seed st.
Bind off in pattern.

FINISHING

Sew Pockets to Front following vertical line of 27th (29th, 31st, 33rd, 35th, 37th) st in from edges so that Pockets will bag slightly. Sew outside edge of Pockets into side seam, set in Sleeves, being careful to sew them into correct sides. Sew on buttons, large ones on front (see drawing), small ones onto cuffs.

artist's satchel

We created this practical bag using a canvas satchel as our model and included a special long inside pocket for extra storage. This is the ideal tote for sketchbooks, brushes, pencils, and paints, but knitters could also use it to carry around their yarn, needles, and patterns.

BODY

Beg with the flap.
With size 6 needles, cast on 111 sts.
Row 1 (RS): K1, *yf, sl 1 p-wise, yb, k1; rep from * to end.
Row 2: P2, *yb, sl 1 purl-wise, yf, p1; rep from * to last st, p1.

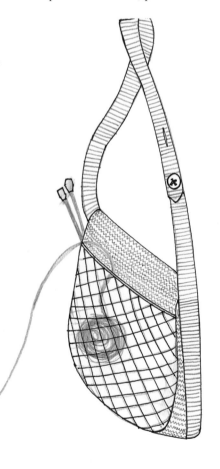

These 2 rows form the patt.
Work in patt for 12½" (32cm).
Next row: Cast on 22 sts for left-hand-side edge of Body, patt to end.
Next row: Cast on 44 sts for right-hand-side edge and inside pocket, patt to end.
Work even for a further 13½" (34cm), with RS facing for next row.
Bind off 22 sts at beg next row, then bind off 44 sts at beg of following row.
Cont in patt for a further 16" (41cm).
Bind off.

STRAP

With size F/5 hook, make chain equal in length to 20 sts' worth of patt.
Work in sc rows until Strap is 82½" (210cm) long.
Make 1 buttonhole in center of strap.
Work a further 2¼" (6cm) in sc.
Fasten off.

FINISHING

Fold the 44 sts at left-hand-side flap in half to wrong side of Body and pin. Bringing right sides together, position so that bound-off edge is level with the tops of the two side flaps, pin and stitch securely down each side to make the Body of the bag, incorporating the side pocket on left-hand side of the bag as you look at it. Stitch Strap around outside of Body, arranging so that button is approximately 6" (15cm) above right-hand side of bag.

Measurements after Washing
Approximately 15" wide x 12" tall (38x30cm), plus Strap

Materials
▶ 13 balls Elann Den-M-Nit (100% cotton, 1¾ oz [50g], 101 yd [92m]) in Ecru
▶ Size 6 (4mm) needles
▶ Size F/5 (4mm) crochet hook

Gauge
27sts and 42 rows = 4" (10cm) using size 6 needles.

Abbreviations and Techniques
Refer to pages 18–19.

CROCHET NET FOR BAG FLAP

With size F/5 hook, make 71 ch.
Foundation Row 1: 1 ss in each ch to end, turn.
Foundation Row 2: 5 ch, skip 2 ss, ss into next ss, *5 chain, skip 2 ss, ss into next ss; rep from * to end.
Patt row: 5 ch, *skip 2 ch, ss into center ch of next 5 ch loop; rep from * to end.
Rep this row until Net measures ¾" (2cm) less than the bag flap.
Work 1 row of sc around side edges and top of Net, then sew onto bag flap along side and bottom edges, leaving top edge open.

50°02′ NORTH, 5°08′ WEST

frenchman's white

Frenchman's Creek refers to a narrow, water-filled valley on the southern coast of Cornwall that runs into the Helford River, not far from the village of Helford. Although locals know the valley as the Frenchman's Pill, Daphne du Maurier popularized the name Frenchman's Creek with her novel of the same name. No one knows for sure how the appellation originated, but one theory refers to a French ship anchored in the creek several centuries ago.

Although it's probably the most well-known creek in Cornwall, Frenchman's is also the most elusive. In fact, because of its seclusion, the creek became a center for undercover operations during World War II. Not surprisingly, Frenchman's Creek can be difficult to find without some advance work. The day that Patrick and I traveled there, it took us two attempts to find it on foot. We suggest that you take a boat from the pier at Helford village.

Nevertheless, a visit is well worth the effort. The creek itself seems otherworldly, its silence broken only by the twitter of birdsong and the snapping of dry twigs underfoot. Shade-loving vegetation lines the banks—ivy, bracken, moss, and lichen. On the shoreline, you can make out sun-bleached petrified trees and their gnarled branches, laced with seaweed, which has drifted to the water's edge. The atmosphere is quite mysterious, but, at the same time, stunning.

We couldn't include a chapter on Frenchman's Creek without providing at least some background on Daphne du Maurier. From a prominent London theatrical family, du Maurier first discovered the Cornish countryside when her father, Gerald, bought a holiday home in the town of

➤ TRANSPORTATION

Helford River Boats: Take the ferry across the Helford River for a visit to the Ferry Boat Inn. Or hire a guide to take you through Frenchman's Creek by boat. www.helford-river-boats.co.uk

Fowey, off the southern coast of Cornwall. It was here, in her Cornish home, that du Maurier began composing short stories as a teenager. Later, when she married a dashing regimental officer named Tommy Browning, the couple decided to spend their honeymoon sailing Tommy's white cabin cruiser from Fowey to Frenchman's Creek, where they anchored at the end of their journey. Du Maurier spent most of her life in Cornwall, where she composed her many bestselling books, including *Jamaica Inn* and *Rebecca*, as well as her short story "The Birds," which Alfred Hitchcock adapted for his cinematic classic.

Du Maurier's 1941 novel, *Frenchman's Creek*, set during the reign of Charles II, describes the creek as a place of

➤ REFRESHMENTS

The Shipwright's Arms: Picturesque thatched-roof pub in Helford village with garden overlooking the Helford River. Serves hearty pub grub and delicious beers.

The Post Office: Helford village post office and sundries store. Sells delicious, organic Roskilly's Cornish ice cream.

The Ferry Boat Inn: Located in Helford Passage, across the river from the Shipwright's Arms. Serves traditional pub food and good beer. Accessible by ferry.

Frenchman's Creek at low tide.

mystery and enchantment. It tells the story of Lady St. Columb, who flees her dull husband and the king's court for a life in Cornwall. The film adaptation of that novel stars Joan Fontaine as Lady St. Columb and Arturo de Cordova as the pirate she falls in love with. Because of World War II, the directors couldn't shoot the movie in England. Instead they headed for Northern California, an area with a similar climate.

The Daphne du Maurier novel inspired the knitwear in this chapter, which is created in ecru yarn and reflects a modern take on a romantic literary setting. To create a lacy, almost ethereal effect, we have used crochet in the Creek Crochet Skirt and open stitchwork in the Lady Dona Ruffle Top.

 GARDENS

Trebah Garden: A subtropical ravine with a unique collection of rare and exotic plants, trees, and shrubs, and its own private beach. Accessible by ferry. www.trebahgarden.co.uk

Glendurgan Gardens: This valley garden in Mawnan Smith near Falmouth offers a sheltered setting for exotic flowers, trees, and shrubs. Accessible by ferry. www.nationaltrust.org.uk

creek crochet skirt

A-line with a tie waist, this skirt's crochet pattern reflects the whimsical history of Frenchman's Creek. Be sure to wear a slip underneath.

Sizes
S–M (M–L, L–XL)

Measurements after Washing
Hip: 38½" (42½", 46½") [98 (108, 118)cm]
Length: 29" (29", 29") [74 (74, 74)cm]

Materials
- 15 (18, 21) balls Elann Den-M-Nit (100% cotton, 1¾ oz [50g], 101 yd [92m]) in Ecru
- Size F/5 (4mm) crochet hook

Gauge
16 dc and 8 rows (dc) = 4" (10cm) square using size F/5 hook before washing.

Abbreviations and Techniques
Refer to pages 18–19.

MOTIF (MAKE 18 (20, 22))

With size F/5 hook, make 6 ch, ss in 1st ch to form a ring.
Round 1: 1 ch, work 16 sc into ring, ss in 1st sc.
Round 2: 6 ch (counts as first 1 dc and 3 ch), skip 2 sts, [1 dc into next st, 3 ch, skip 1 st] 7 times, ss in 3rd of 6 ch.
Round 3: 1 ch, work a petal of [1 sc, 1 hdc, 5 dc, 1 hdc, 1 sc] into each of next eight 3-ch arches, ss to 1st dc.
Round 4: Behind petals of Round 3, work [6 ch, 1 sc between 2 sc on Round 3] 7 times, 6 ch, 1 sc in ss on Round 3.
Fasten off.
Round 5: Ch, work a petal of [1 sc, 1 hdc, 6 dc, 1 hdc, 1 sc] into each of next eight 6-ch arches, ss to 1st sc.
Round 6: Ss in next hdc and each of next 2 dc, 1 ch, 1 sc in same place as last ss, *[4 ch, skip 2 dc, 1 sc in next dc, 4 ch, 1 sc onto 2nd dc of next petal] twice, 6 ch, 1 sc onto 2nd dc of next petal; rep from * twice more, [4 ch, skip 2 dc, 1 sc in next dc, 4 ch, 1 sc onto 2nd dc of next petal] twice, 3 ch, 1 dc in 1st sc.
Round 7: 3 ch, 3 dc in round dc of previous round, *[2 ch, 1 sc in next 4-ch lp, [4 ch, 1 sc in next 4-ch lp] twice, 2 ch, [4 dc, 4 ch, 4 dc] all in next 6-ch lp; rep from * twice more, [2 ch, 1 sc in next 4-ch lp, [4 ch, 1 sc in next 4-ch lp] twice, 2 ch, 4 dc in next lp, 4 ch, ss in 3rd of 3 ch.
Fasten off.

TIER 1

Start at waist.
With size F/5 hook, make 114 (125, 136) ch.
Foundation row (WS): Skip 3 ch, 1 dc in each next ch, *1 dc in each ch to end, turn—112 (123, 134) sts.
Cont in patt:
Row 1: 3 ch, skip 1st dc, 1 dc in each dc to end, 1 dc in 3rd of 3 ch, turn.
Row 2: 3 ch, skip 1st dc, 1 dc in each of next 5 dc, [2 dc in next dc, 1 dc in each of next 10 dc] 9 (10, 11) times, 2 dc in next dc, 1 dc each of next 5 dc, 1 dc in top of 3 ch, turn—122 (134, 146) sts.
Row 3: 3 ch, skip 1st dc, 1 dc in each dc to end, 1 dc in 3rd of 3 ch, turn.
Row 4: 3 ch, skip 1st dc, 1 dc in each of next 6 dc, [2 dc in next dc, 1 dc in each of next 11 dc] 9 (10, 11) times, 2 dc in next dc, 1 dc in each of next 5 dc, 1 dc in top of 3 ch, turn—132 (145, 158) sts.
Row 5: 3 ch, skip 1st dc, 1 dc in each dc to end, 1 dc in 3rd of 3 ch, turn.
Row 6: 3 ch, skip 1st dc, 1 dc in each of next 6 dc, [2 dc in next dc, 1 dc in each of next 12 dc] 9 (10,11) times, 2 dc in next dc, 1 dc each of next 6 dc, 1 dc in top of 3 ch, turn—142 (156, 170) sts.
Row 7: 3 ch, skip 1st dc, 1 dc in each dc to end, 1 dc in 3rd of 3 ch, turn.
Row 8: 3 ch, skip 1st tr, 1 dc in each of next 7 dc, [2 dc in next dc, 1 dc in each of next 13 dc] 9 (10, 11) times, 2 tr in next dc, 1 dc each of next 6 dc,

Total length = 3" (7.4 cm)
½ hem width = 45½" (116 cm)
½ waist width = 13¾" (35 cm)
Length of ties = 12½" (32 cm)
Width of ties = ¼" (.5 cm)
½ Hip width = 19" (48 cm)
Slit depth at side of waist = 4" (10 cm)

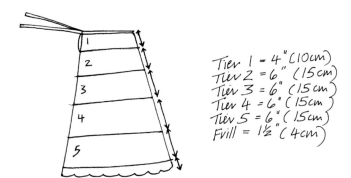

Tier 1 = 4" (10 cm)
Tier 2 = 6" (15 cm)
Tier 3 = 6" (15 cm)
Tier 4 = 6" (15 cm)
Tier 5 = 6" (15 cm)
Frill = 1½" (4 cm)

1 dc in top of 3 ch, turn—152 (167, 182) sts.
Row 9: 3 ch, skip 1st dc, 1 tr in each dc to end, 1 dc in 3rd of 3 ch, turn.

TIER 2
Join 8 (9, 10) motifs into a strip. Join 1 long edge to last row of dc.

TIER 3
With size F/5 hook, make 164 (180, 196) ch.
Foundation row (WS): Skip 3 ch, 1 dc in each next ch, *1 dc in each ch to end, turn—162 (178, 194) sts.
Cont in patt:
Row 1: 3 ch, skip 1st dc, 1 dc in each dc to end, 1 dc in 3rd of 3 ch, turn.
Rows 2 and 3: As Row 1.
Row 4: 3 ch, skip 1st dc, 1 dc in each of next 8 dc, [2 dc in next dc, 1 dc in each of next 15 dc] 9 (10, 11) times, 2 dc in next dc, 1 dc each of next 7 dc, 1 dc in top of 3 ch, turn—172 (189, 206) sts.
Rows 5–8: As Row 1.
Row 9: 3 ch, skip 1st dc, 1 dc in each of next 8 dc, [2 dc in next dc, 1 dc in each of next 16 dc] 9 (10, 11) times, 2 dc in next dc, 1 dc each of next 8 dc, 1 dc in top of 3 ch, turn—182 (200, 218) sts.
Rows 10–13: As Row 1.
Row 14: 3 ch, miss 1st dc, 1 dc in each of next 9 dc, [2 dc in next dc, 1 dc in each of next 17 dc] 9 (10, 11) times, 2 dc in next dc, 1 dc each of next 8 dc, 1 dc in top of 3 ch, turn—192 (211, 230) sts.
Fasten off.

TIER 4
Join 10 (11, 12) motifs into a strip. Join one long edge to last row of dc.

TIER 5
With size F/5 hook, make 204 (224, 244) ch.
Foundation row (WS): Skip 3 ch, 1 dc in each next ch, *1 dc in each ch to end, turn—202 (222, 242) sts.
Cont in patt:

Row 1: 3 ch, skip 1st dc, 1 dc in each dc to end, 1 dc in 3rd of 3 ch, turn.

Rows 2 and 3: As Row 1.

Row 4: 3 ch, skip 1st dc, 1 dc in each of next 10 dc, [2 dc in next dc, 1 dc in each of next 19 dc] 9 (10, 11) times, 2 dc in next dc, 1 dc each of next 9 dc, 1 dc in top of 3 ch, turn—212 (233, 254) sts.

Rows 5–8: As Row 1.

Row 9: 3 ch, skip 1st dc, 1 dc in each of next 10 dc, [2 dc in next dc, 1 dc in each of next 20 dc] 9 times, 2 dc in next dc, 1 dc in each of next 10 dc, 1 dc in top of 3 ch, turn—222 (244, 266) sts.

Rows 10–13: As Row 1.

Row 14: 3 ch, skip 1st dc, 1 dc in each of next 11 dc, [2 dc in next dc, 1 dc in each of next 21 dc] 9 (10, 11) times, 2 dc in next dc, 1 dc each of next 10 dc, 1 dc in top of 3 ch, turn—232 (255, 278) sts.

S–M size only

Row 15: 1 ch, skip 1st dc, 1 sc in each dc to end, 1 sc in 3rd of 3 ch, turn—231 sc.

M–L/L–XL sizes only

Row 15: 1 ch, skip 1st dc, 1 sc in each of next (1, 0) dc, [2 sc in next dc, 1 sc in each of next (41, 91) dc] (6, 3) times, 1 sc in 3rd of 3 ch, turn—(261, 281) sc.

All sizes

Row 16: 1 ch, 1 sc in 1st sc, 2 ch, skip 2 sc, 1 sc in next sc, 8 ch, skip 3 sc, 1 sc in next sc, *5 ch, skip 5 sc, 1 sc in next sc, 8 ch, skip 3 sc, 1 sc in next sc; rep from * to last 3 sc, 2 ch, 1 sc in last sc, turn.

Row 17: 1 ch, 1 sc in 1st sc, 19 dc in 8 ch arch, *1 sc in next 5-ch sp, 19 dc in 8-ch arch; rep from * to last 2-ch sp, 1 sc in last sc.
Fasten off.

TIES (MAKE 2)

With size F/5 hook, make 64 ch, miss 1st ch, 1 sc in each ch to end.
Fasten off.

FINISHING

Join Tier 3 to Tier 2 and Tier 5 to Tier 4. Join side seam from top of Tier 2 to hem. Attach Ties to waist.

lady dona ruffle top

With its long sleeves and relaxed fit, this top is as comfortable as it is romantic. The body is knit on size 10½ (7mm) needles while the voluminous ruffled collar calls for a size 6 (4mm) pair. I recommend wearing a Lycra shell underneath.

Sizes
XS (S, M, L, XL, XXL)

Measurements after Washing
Chest: 34" (36¼", 38½", 41, 43¼", 45½") [86 (92, 98, 104, 110, 116)cm]
Length to shoulder: 23½" (23½", 24, 24½", 24½") [60 (60, 61, 61, 62, 62)cm]
Sleeve length: 16½" (17", 17¼", 17¼", 17¾", 17¾") [42 (43, 44, 44, 45, 45)cm]

Materials
▶ 8 (8, 9, 10, 10, 11) balls Rowan Denim (100% cotton, 1¾ oz [50g], 108 yd [93m]) in Ecru
▶ Size 10½ (7mm) needles
▶ Size 6 (4mm) circular needle

Gauge
11½ sts and 14½ rows = 4" (10cm) in st st with size 10½ needles before washing.

Abbreviations and Techniques
Refer to pages 18–19.

BACK
With size 10½ needles, cast on 48 (54, 60, 66, 72, 78) sts.
Beg with a k row, cont in st st.
Work in 20 (20, 22, 22, 24, 24) rows.
Next row: K2, ssk, k to last 4 sts, k2tog, k2.
Work 19 rows.
Next row: K2, ssk, k to last 4 sts, k2tog, k2—44 (50, 56, 62, 68, 74) sts.
Cont in st st until 60 (60, 62, 62, 64, 64) rows have been worked**.

Shape armholes
Bind off 1 st at beg of next 4 (6, 8, 10, 12, 14) rows—40 (44, 48, 52, 56, 60) sts.
Work a further 22 rows in st st.

Shape shoulders
Bind off 4 (5, 5, 6, 6, 7) sts at beg of next 2 rows—5 (5, 6, 6, 7, 7) sts at beg of foll 2 rows.
Bind off rem 22 (24, 26, 28, 30, 32) sts.

FRONT
Work as given for Back to **.

Shape armholes and neck
Next row: Bind off 1 st at beg of next row, k until there are 21 (24, 27, 30, 33, 36) sts on right-hand needle, turn, working on these sts only for left side of Front neck.
Next row: P1, p2tog, p to end.
Next row: Bind off 1, k to end.
Rep the last 2 rows 0 (1, 2, 3, 4, 5) times.

Next row: P1, p2tog, p to end.
Next row: K to end.
Rep the last 2 rows until 9 (10, 11, 12, 13, 14) sts rem.
P 1 row.

Shape shoulder
Bind off 4 (5, 5, 6, 6, 7) sts at beg of next row.
Work 1 row.
Bind off rem 5 (5, 6, 6, 7, 7) sts.
With right side facing, rejoin yarn to rem sts, k to end.
Complete to match 1st side of neck shaping.

SLEEVES (MAKE 2)
With size 10½ needles, cast on 24 (26, 28, 30, 32, 34) sts.
Beg with a k row, cont in st st.
Work in 6 (6, 8, 8, 10, 10) rows.
Next row: K2, m1, k to last 2 sts, m1, k2.
Work 5 rows.
Rep the last 6 rows until there are 44 (46, 48, 50, 52, 54) sts.
Work even until 74 (74, 76, 76, 78, 78) rows have been worked.

Shape Sleeve top
Bind off 2 sts at beg of next 2 rows.
Next row: K2, k2tog, k to last 4 sts, ssk, k2.
Next row: P to end.
Rep the last 2 rows 6 (6, 7, 7, 8, 8) times more.
Next row: K2, slip 1, k2tog, psso, k to last 5 sts, slip 1, skpo, psso, k2.

Next row: P to end.
Rep the last 2 rows twice more—14 (16, 16, 18, 18, 20) sts.
Bind off.

RUFFLE

With size 6 circular needle and the long-tail cast-on method, cast on 421 sts.
Row 1: K1, *p1, k1; rep from * to end.
Row 2: P1, *k1, p1; rep from * to end.
Rep these 2 rows 4 times more.
Row 11: *K1, p1, k1, drop next st rep from * to last st, k1—316 sts.
Rows 12 and 13: Work in rib as set.
Row 14: *K1, p1, k1, drop next st rep from * to end—237 sts.
Row 15: *K2tog, rep to last st, k1.
Bind off.

FINISHING

Join shoulder seams. Set in Sleeves.
Join side and sleeve seams.
Slip st Ruffle into place around neck, starting and ending at point of V, leaving ruffle ends open. Unravel dropped ruffle stitches.

frenchman's blue slippers

While the slippers shown here are crocheted in three colors, they would look equally good in one solid color. You could also decorate them with beads or embroider them.

Sizes
XS (S, M, L)
Corresponds approximately to women's American sizes 5½ (7½, 8½, 9½)

Materials
▶ 1 ball Elann Den-M-Nit (100% cotton, 1¾ oz [50g], 101 yd [92m]) in Mid indigo (A), 1 ball in Light Indigo (B), and 1 ball in Ecru (C)
▶ Size F/5 (4mm) crochet hook
▶ Sewing needle and thread

Gauge
36 sts (2 patt reps) and 5 rows plus foundation row = 7¾" (19.5cm) wide and 3¼" (8cm) deep using size F/5 hook before washing.

Abbreviations and Techniques
Refer to pages 18–19.

SOLE

With size F/5 hook and A, make 21 ch.
Round 1: 5 sc in 2nd ch from hook, 1 sc in each of next 18 ch, 5 sc in last ch, then working along other side of ch, work 1 sc in each of next 18 ch, 1 sc in 1st ch.
Round 2: Mark sc at center of both ends, *1 sc in each sc to marked sc, 5 sc in next sc; rep from * once more, 1 sc in each sc, 1 sc in 1st sc.
Rep the last round 3 (4, 5, 6) times more.
Next round: 1 sc in each sc, ss in 1st sc.
Rep the last round 1 (2, 3, 3) times more.
Fasten off.

UPPER

Motif (Make 5)

Round 1: Wrap C around finger once to form a ring, 3 ch, 15 dc into ring, pull ring tight, ss in 3rd of 3 ch. Fasten off.
Round 2: Attach B to any space between dc, 1 sc in same place as join, *skip 2 sts, 6 dc in next sp between sts, skip 2 sts, 1 sc in next sp between sts; rep from * omitting 1 sc at end of last rep, ss in 1st sc. Fasten off.

XS size only

Round 3: Mark 2 dc at center of each of the 4 corners. Attach C to 1st dc after marked dc, 2 ch, *1 hdc in each dc to marked dc, 3 hdc in each of next dc; rep from * ending ss in top of 2 ch. Fasten off.
Round 4: Attach A to any hdc, 1 sc into each hdc, ss in 1st sc. Fasten off.

S, M, L size only

Round 3: Mark 2 dc at center of each of the 4 corners. Attach C to 1st dc after marked dc, 3 ch, *1 dc in each dc to marked dc, 4 dc in each of next 2 dc; rep from * ending ss in top of 3 ch. Fasten off.
Round 4: Attach A to any dc, 1 sc into each dc, ss in 1st sc. Fasten off.

M, L size only

Mark sc at each corner.
Round 5: Attach B to any sc, *1 sc into each sc until marked sc, 3 sc into marked sc, rep from * ending ss into lst sc.
Repeat this round once more for Large size.

FINISHING

Join the 1st 4 motifs into a strip. Insert remaining motif, joining one side to end of strip and adjacent side to beginning of strip.
Sew widest edge of Upper to Sole.

Edging

With right side facing, attach A to any sc, *1 sc in each of next 3 sts, 3 ch, 1 sc in same place as last sc; rep from *, ss in 1st sc. Fasten off.

50°13′ NORTH, 5°28′ WEST

st. ives blue

St. Ives lies on the northwest end of St. Ives Bay, approximately twenty minutes by car from Land's End, the most southwesterly tip of the UK. The name *St. Ives* is steeped in legend; it probably refers to St. Ia, the fifth-century Irish princess and Christian missionary who, according to local lore, sailed from Ireland to St. Ives on a leaf. She founded an oratory on the site of the present-day parish church.

The best way to reach St. Ives is by train. Start from London's Paddington or Penzance Station and catch the connecting train from St. Erth to St. Ives. This is one of the most beautiful stretches of railway in the country, hugging the cliffs along the north coast and giving you a panoramic view of St. Ives Bay and the ocean beyond. After the penultimate stop at Carbis Bay, the little connector train emerges from a valley to reveal the picture-postcard town of St. Ives, which also boasts a wealth of art galleries, a surfing beach, and some excellent restaurants, bars, and shops.

Life in St. Ives has always centered around the harbor and its sandy beaches. The town itself is reminiscent of a Greek fishing village, with its steep hills, wonderful labyrinthine alleyways, and steps that all seem to lead down to the water's edge. St. Ives is also renowned for its quasi-Mediterranean light, which is almost surreal in its clarity.

St. Ives was originally a fishing village. While some fishing still goes on here, tourism is now the predominant industry. Nevertheless, its fishing history has shaped the town. The area around the harbor is called Down-a-long (pronounced as one word), which was once a very poor and rundown area, populated by fishermen. The people from Up-a-long (the professional classes who lived at the top of the hill) preferred not to venture there. Today, the fishermen's cottages in the Down-a-long area predominately consist of immaculate vacation homes.

Although renowned for its beauty and its excellent surfing beaches, St. Ives is best known as an artists' colony. In the late nineteenth century, it became a fashionable destination for artists from all over the UK, as well as some American and Scandinavian artists. Both J. M. W. Turner and James McNeill Whistler came to paint here. But the town is famous for its ties to the Abstract Art Movement, which became popular in the late 1950s and early '60s. The first wave of abstract artists arrived in St. Ives just after the outbreak of World War II. This wave included Adrian

A winding back street in St. Ives.

Stokes, Margaret Mellis, Ben Nicholson, Bernard Leach (who came to St. Ives after studying in Japan), and Barbara Hepworth, later to be joined by the Russian-born Gabo. After these pioneers, second and third waves followed suit. Some of these artists (from Cornwall and elsewhere) include Alfred Wallis, John Wells, Denis Mitchell, Peter Lanyon, Sir Terry Frost, Wilhelmina Barnes-Graham, Roger Hilton, Patrick Heron, Sandra Blow, Ken Symonds, Antony Frost, and Kurt Jackson.

While all these artists have solid reputations in their own right, Hepworth is perhaps the most famous. Hepworth is best known for her carvings in bronze, marble, slate, and stone. Today, St. Ives is home to the Barbara Hepworth Museum. The museum displays her work in her studio and in a lush outdoor subtropical garden. In her stone carving workshop, everything is preserved just as it was—her materials and tools are still laid out, even her overalls hang on the wall.

Another must-see in this region is the Tate Gallery St. Ives. Opened in 1993 by His Royal Highness Prince Charles, the gallery is built on the old gasworks and includes a light-filled café at the top, with superb views of Porthmeor Beach, one of the most stunning beaches in Cornwall. And you might be rewarded, as I once was, by the sight of dolphins dancing in perfect synchronized formation.

The projects in this chapter are inextricably linked to the Abstract Art Movement. In fact, we've based the handknitting for these projects on abstract pattern design using a method of knitting known as intarsia, as seen in both the Abstract Art Cushion (page 102) and the Abstract Art Sweater (page 98). Intarsia knitting allows you to knit with more than one color of yarn in a row without having to strand colors across the back of the work, as in Fair Isle knitting. This technique is used when the distance between the color changes is greater than four to five stitches and a single thickness of fabric is required. Although many knitters are somewhat apprehensive about intarsia work, it is actually very easy to do once you know how. It simply requires that a separate ball or strand of yarn be used for each part of the design that requires a color change. At the change point on each row, the two yarns (the one just knitted with and the next color to be used) are twisted around each other so that a hole does not develop.

abstract art sweater

This sweater features an intarsia front, a plain black back, and ribbed sleeves. The abstract art design was inspired by the St. Ives modernist movement that made headlines in the 1950s.

FRONT

With size 3 needles and A, cast on 108 (114, 122, 132, 144, 156) sts. K 9 rows. Change to size 6 needles.
Cont in st st and rev st st following the chart for color changes, working shapings as shown.
Bind off.

BACK

With size 3 needles and A, cast on 108 (114, 122, 132, 144, 156) sts. K 9 rows. Change to size 6 needles.
Cont in st st following the chart, working shapings as shown.
Bind off.

SLEEVES (MAKE 2)

With size 4 needles and A, cast on 46 (50, 54, 62, 66, 70) sts.
Row 1: K2, *p2, k2; rep from * to end.
Row 2: P2, *k2, p2; rep from * to end.
These 2 rows set the rib patt.
Work a further 8 rows.
Row 11: K2, m1, rib to last 2 sts, m1, k2.
Work 9 rows even.
Rep the last 10 rows until there are 66 (70, 74, 82, 86, 90) rows, making inc sts into rib. Work even until 118 (118, 120, 120, 124, 124) rows have been worked in total.

Shape Sleeve top

Bind off 3 (4, 5, 6, 7, 8) sts at beg of next 2 rows then 2 sts at beg of foll 6 rows—48 (50, 52, 58, 60, 62) sts.
Dec 1 st at each end of the next and 2 foll alt rows.
Work 5 rows even.
Dec 1 st at each end of the next row.
Work 7 rows even.
Dec 1 st at each end of the next row.
Work 5 rows even.
Bind off 2 sts at beg of next 2 rows.
Work 2 rows even.
Bind off 2 sts at beg of next 2 rows.
Rep the last 4 rows 2 (2, 2, 3, 3, 3) times more.
Bind off 3 sts at beg of next 2 rows.
Bind off.

NECKBAND

Join right shoulder. With right side facing and size 3 needles, pick up and k 20 sts down left Front neck, 20 (22, 24, 26, 28, 30) sts across center Front neck, 20 sts up right Front neck, 46 (48, 50, 52, 54, 56) sts across Back neck—106 (110, 114, 118, 122, 126) sts.
Row 1: K2, *p2, k2; rep from * to end.
Row 2: P2, *k2, p2; rep from * to end.
Rep these 2 rows until neckband measures 1⅜" (3.5cm).
Bind off.

FINISHING

Join left shoulder and neckband. Join side seams, join sleeve seams, and set in Sleeves.

Sizes

XS (S, M, L, XL, XXL)

Measurements after Washing

Chest: 36¼" (38½", 41¾", 45¾", 50½", 55") [92 (98, 106, 116, 128, 140)cm]
Length to shoulder: 24" (24½", 24¾", 25¼", 25½", 26") [61 (62, 63, 64, 65, 66)cm]
Sleeve length: 17" (17, 17¼", 17¼", 17¾", 17¾") [43 (43, 44, 44, 45, 45)cm]

Materials

- ▶ 11 (13, 15, 17, 19, 21) balls Rowan Handknit Cotton DK (100% cotton, 1¾ oz [50g], 93 yd [85m]) in Black (A)
- ▶ 3 (3, 3, 5, 5, 5) balls Rowan Denim (100% cotton, 1¾ oz [50g], 108 yd [93m]) in 229 Memphis (B)
- ▶ Size 3 (3.25mm) needles
- ▶ Size 6 (4mm) needles
- ▶ Size 4 (3.5mm) needles

Gauge

Handknit Cotton: 20 sts and 28 rows = 4" (10cm) square in XXL2 rib using size 4 needles, when very slightly stretched out.
Denim: 20 sts and 28 rows = 4" (10cm) square in st st using size 6 needles before washing.

Abbreviations and Techniques

Refer to pages 18–19.

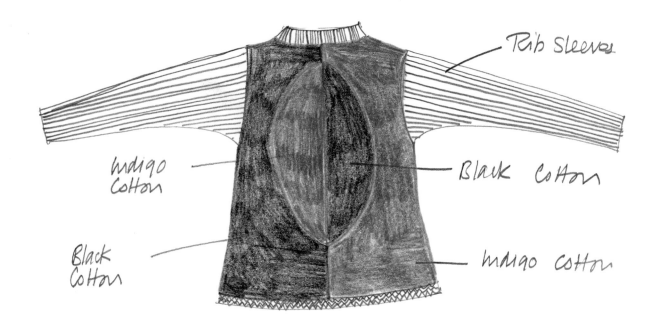

Rib Sleeves

Indigo Cotton

Black Cotton

Black Cotton

Indigo Cotton

ST. IVES BARS

The Hub: Hip bar with retro décor. Good sea views from the first floor. Located on the Wharf.

Pedn-Olva Hotel: Offers stunning views of St. Ives in the evening. Located on the Warren.

The Sloop Inn: You can't do better for atmosphere than this fourteenth-century inn made famous by fishermen and artists. The Cellar Bar, at the back of the inn, features an ever-changing exhibition of paintings by the teachers and students from the St. Ives School of painting, all of which are for sale. www.sloop-inn.co.uk

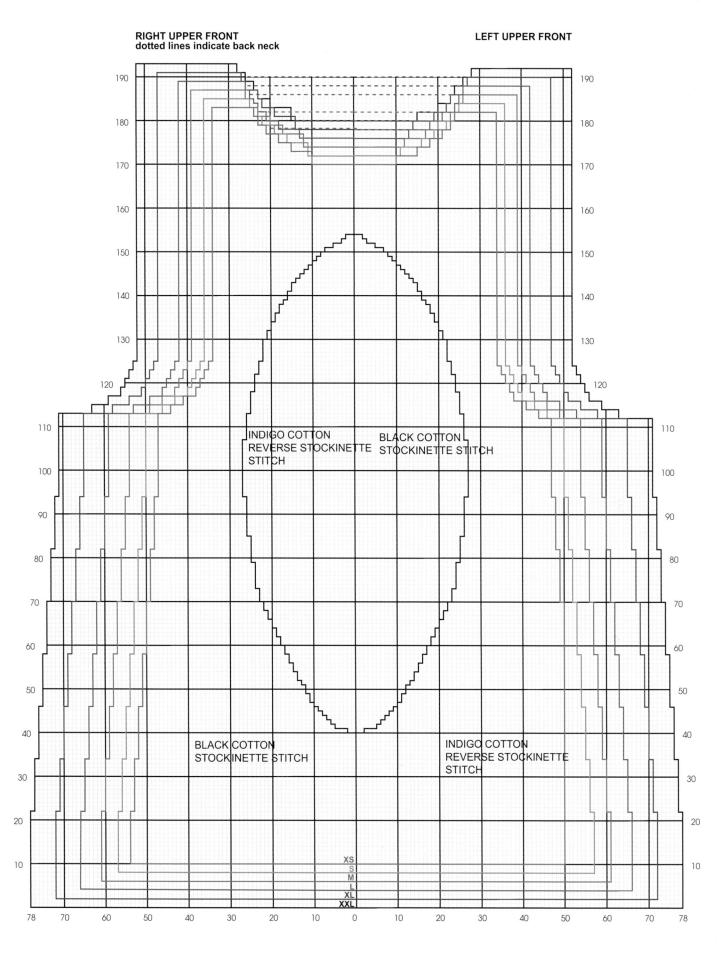

RIGHT UPPER FRONT
dotted lines indicate back neck

LEFT UPPER FRONT

INDIGO COTTON
REVERSE STOCKINETTE
STITCH

BLACK COTTON
STOCKINETTE STITCH

BLACK COTTON
STOCKINETTE STITCH

INDIGO COTTON
REVERSE STOCKINETTE
STITCH

XS
S
M
L
XL
XXL

abstract art cushion

Measurements after Washing
Approximately 23$\frac{2}{3}$"
(60cm) square

This cushion is large, so I suggest you use it for the floor. The front features an abstract design influenced by the St. Ives modernist movement. A mitered border completes the look.

Materials
- 12 balls Rowan Denim (100% cotton, 1¾ oz [50g], 108 yd [93m]) in Ecru (A), 2 balls in Nashville (B), 2 balls in Memphis (C), and 2 balls in Tennessee (D)
- Size 6 (4mm) needles
- Size 3 (3.25mm) needles
- Size 5 (3.75mm) needles
- Size 3 (3.25mm) circular needles
- Stitch markers
- Sewing needle and thread
- 3 large buttons

Gauge
20 sts and 28 rows = 4" (10cm) square in st st using size 6 needles before washing.

Abbreviations and Techniques
Refer to pages 18–19.

Note
When working motif, use intarsia. Separate balls of yarn for each part of the chart and twist yarns on wrong side when changing color to avoid a hole.

FRONT
With size 6 needles and D, cast on 120 sts.
Following chart, work in st st for 174 rows.
Bind off.

BACK

Piece 1
With size 3 needles and A, cast on 120 sts.
K21 rows.
Change to size 6 needles.
Starting with a k row, work 120 rows in st st.
Bind off.

Piece 2
With size 5 needles and C, cast on 121 sts.
K13 rows.
Buttonhole Row 1: K28, [bind off 3 sts, k next 27 sts] 3 times.
Buttonhole Row 2: K to end, cast on 3 sts over those bind off in previous row.
K6 rows.
Change to size 6 needles.
Starting with a k row, work 53 rows in st st.
Row 54: P60, p2tog, p to end— 120 sts.
Bind off.

MITERED BORDER
With right side of Front facing, size 3 circular needle, and A, pick up and k120 across bind-off row, mark first st, pick up and k116 down side of cushion, mark first st, pick up and k120 across bottom with 2nd circular needle, mark 1st st, and 116 sts up remaining side, mark 1st st—472 sts.
Round 1 (RS): P to end.
Round 2: K1, m1, *k to next marked corner st, m1, k the marked st, m1; rep from * twice more, k to end, m1. 8 sts inc—480 sts.
Round 3: P to end.
Round 4: As Round 2—488 sts.
Cont in this way, increasing either side of the corner st on every k row until a total of 21 rounds have been worked—552 sts.
Round 22: K1, k2tog, *k to 2 sts before next corner st, skpo, k1, k2tog; rep from * twice more, k to last 2 sts of round, skpo. 8 sts dec—544 sts.
Round 23: P to end.
Cont in this way, decreasing either side of the corner st on every k row until 472 sts rem.
P1 round.
Bind off loosely.

FINISHING
Fold border over. With wrong sides together, pin Backs onto Front, with miter-bind-off edge on top. With D, running stitch neatly through all 3 layers to hold cushion together, 1 running st per knitted st. Sew on buttons.

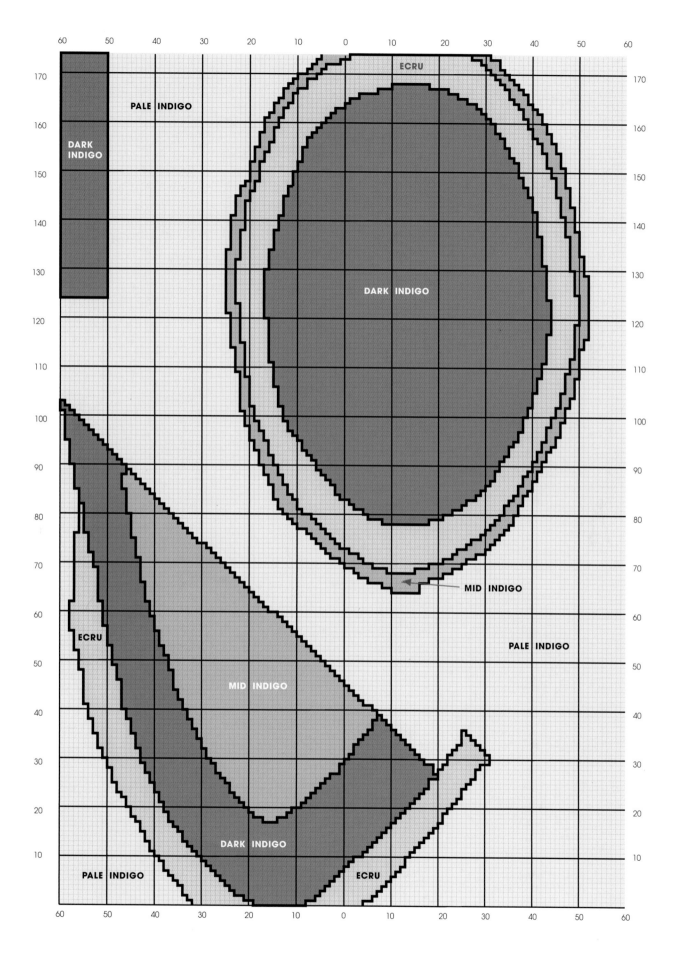

painterly stripe sweater

This modern sweater is first knit in a series of narrow stripes. The circular fade is then created by tracing a circle around a bowl with bleach solution (instructions on page 14). This look always reminds me of a painting that has been left out too long in the sun.

Sizes
S (M, L, XL)

Measurements after Washing
Chest: 41¾" (45¾", 49¾", 53½") [106 (116, 126, 136)cm]
Length to shoulder: 23½" (24, 24¾", 25¼") [60 (61, 63, 64)cm]
Sleeve length: 19¼" (19¾", 20, 20½") [49 (50, 51, 52)cm]

Materials
- 3 (3, 4, 4) balls Rowan Denim (100% cotton, 1¾ oz [50g], 108 yd [93m]) each in Nashville (A), Memphis (B), Tennessee (C), and Ecru (D)
- 5 (5, 6, 6) balls Rowan Handknit Cotton DK (100% cotton, 1¾ oz [50g], 93 yd [85m]) in Black (E)
- Size 5 (3.75mm) needles
- Size 6 (4mm) needles
- Stitch holders

Gauge
20 sts and 28 rows = 4" (10cm) square in st st using size 6 needles before washing.

Abbreviations and Techniques
Refer to pages 18–19.

STRIPE SEQUENCE
2 rows each B, A, B, C, D, B, D, E, A, C, D, C, E, B, A, C, A, D, E, and B. These 40 rows form the stripe sequence.

BACK
With size 5 needles and E, cast on 106 (116, 126, 136) sts.
Working in stripe patt, k4 rows.
Change to size 6 needles.
Cont in st st and stripe pattern. Work 118 (120, 124, 126) rows.

Shape armholes
Dec 1 st each end of next and every foll 4th row until 80 (90, 100, 110) sts rem**.
Work even until 186 (190, 196, 200) rows have been worked in total.

Shape shoulders
Bind off 6 (7, 8, 9) sts at beg of next 6 rows.
Leave rem 44 (48, 52, 56) sts on a spare needle.

FRONT
Work as given for Back to **.
Work 7 (11, 17, 21) rows even.
174 (178, 184, 188) rows have been worked. (Note which stripe row you are on for neckband.)

Shape neck
Next row: K28 (32, 36, 40), turn and work on these sts only for left side of neck.

Next row: Bind off 3 (4, 5, 6) sts at beg of this row.
Work 1 row.
Bind off 3 sts at beg of next row and 2 sts on foll alt row.
Work 1 row.
Dec 1 st at beg of next and foll alt row—18 (21, 24, 27) sts.
Work 2 rows even.

Shape shoulder
Bind off 6 (7, 8, 9) sts at beg of next and foll alt row.
Work 1 row.
Bind off rem 6 (7, 8, 9) sts.
With right side facing, slip next 24 (26, 28, 30) sts onto a holder, rejoin yarn to remaining sts, k to end.
Complete right side to match left.

SLEEVES (MAKE 2)
With size 5 needles and E, cast on 44 (48, 52, 56) sts.
Work first 4 rows of stripe patt in garter st.
Change to size 6 needles and work in st st, and stripe patt.
Work 4 rows.
Inc row: K2, m1, k to last 2 sts, m1, k2.
Work 5 rows.
Rep the last 6 rows until there are 80 (86, 92, 98) sts.
Work even until 154 (160, 166, 172) rows have been worked.

Shape top
Dec 1 st at each end of next and every
foll alt row until there are 30 sts.
P1 row.
Bind off.

NECKBAND
Join right shoulder seam.
With right side facing, size 5 needles,
and correct color to carry on stripe
patt at center Front, pick up and k19
sts down left Front neck, k24 (26, 28,
30) sts from front neck holder, pick
up and k19 sts up right side of neck, k
across 44 (48, 52, 56) sts on Back
neck holder—106 (112, 118, 124) sts.
Working in stripe patt, k4 rows.
Bind off loosely.

FINISHING
Join left shoulder seam and neckband.
Sew Sleeves into armhole shapings on
body, and join side and sleeve seams.

ST. IVES ART

**Barbara Hepworth Museum and Sculpture
Garden:** A very personal look inside this legendary
sculptor's studio. www.tate.org.uk/stives/hepworth

Leach Pottery: New project displaying works
from the celebrated potter Bernard Leach.
Features his wonderful Japanese-inspired pots.
www.leachproject.co.uk

Penwith Gallery and Print Workshop: Once a
pilchard cellar, now the home of the Penwith
Society of Artists, founded by Ben Nicholson and
Barbara Hepworth. Exhibits include works from
established artists as well as newcomers. Located
on Back Road West.

St. Ives Ceramics: An amazing collection of studio
pottery, both classic and contemporary, by national
and international potters. www.st-ives-ceramic.co.uk

St. Ives School of Painting: Offers a wide range of
courses in painting and drawing, including a
weekly Life Drawing class, which is open to people
of all skill levels. Just try not to get distracted by
the mesmerizing view of Porthmeor Beach!
www.stivesartschool.co.uk

St. Ives Society of Artists: Formed in 1927, this
society has included among its members Stanhope
Forbes, Ben Nicholson, Barbara Hepworth, and
Peter Lanyon. www.stivessocietyofartists.com

Tate Gallery St. Ives: Overlooking Porthmeor
Beach, where surfers ride the waves below the
gallery, this is an amazing place to see the fusion of
art and sport. www.tate.org.uk/stives

Tremayne Applied Arts: A gallery selling furniture,
prints, ceramics, glass, and clothing—from art
deco to Bauhaus and modernism, as well as
pieces from the 1950s and '60s. Located on Street
An Pol.

A few other notable galleries: Belgrave Gallery,
Cornerstone Gallery, New Craftsman, the New
Millennium Gallery, Penhaven Gallery, Plumbline
Gallery, Porthminster Gallery, Printmaker's Gallery,
Salthouse Gallery, Waterside Gallery, and Will's
Lane Gallery.

49°57' NORTH, 6°20' WEST

tresco blue

Tresco is one of the five inhabited islands that make up the Isles of Scilly. The islands lie twenty-eight miles (45km) west by southwest of mainland Cornwall, and in addition to the five inhabited islands, the archipelago consists of fifty-one uninhabited land masses. To the west of Tresco, there is the island of Bryher, to the east St. Martin's, and to the south the islands of St. Agnes and St. Mary's.

Surrounded by clear, turquoise seas and white shell beaches, Tresco feels much more exotic than other parts of the UK. Because the island is car-free, pollution is virtually nonexistent. Residents and tourists get around on bicycles and golf carts, and tractors pull trailers of visitors along. The two main attractions on the island are the exquisite coastal scenery and the magnificent Abbey Gardens, which are a horticulturist's paradise, full of subtropical plants, shrubs, and trees gathered from around the world. Tresco is also a wonderful base for walking, bird-watching, and observing marine life. At certain times of the year you can spot dolphins, porpoises, seals, and basking sharks.

The Abbey Gardens were created by the extraordinary vision of a man named Augustus Smith. Without his gardens, Tresco would be a rather windswept and barren place, supporting only gorse bushes and other vegetation that could thrive despite the wild ocean storms brought in by the Atlantic. Smith, who in 1834 procured a lease over the Isles of Scilly from the Duchy of Cornwall, chose Tresco as the site of his garden for two reasons. First, the other nearby islands sheltered it from the elements, and second, it has a remarkably warm climate, due to both the Gulf Stream. Smith realized that if he could also shelter Tresco from ocean storms, it could be a superb place to plant an exotic garden.

Smith came up with the idea of building twelve-foot (11m) stone walls to the west of the island and slightly lower ones to the east. To test how well his walls would protect the land from ocean storms, he then had exotic plants delivered from the Royal Botanical Gardens at Kew Gardens in London. Smith soon discovered that the most

Tresco is one of the five in habited islands southwest of mainland Cornwall.

successful plants came from Australia, New Zealand, and South Africa. He also realized that he was going to need something more substantial than high walls to shield his new garden, so he introduced Monterey pine and cypress from the Monterey Peninsula of California. These trees did the job beautifully, and the foundations were now laid for one of the most visionary gardens in the UK, if not the world.

Since Smith's death in 1872, the gardens have been handed down through five generations. Smith's nephew, Thomas Algernon Dorrieu-Smith, was responsible for introducing flower growing to the Isles of Scilly. This trade

The ferry arriving on Tresco.

soon became very profitable, since the islands, with their earlier, milder springs, have at least a month's advantage over the mainland. The main crop was (and still is) daffodils.

In addition to its exquisite horticulture, the island of Tresco has many beautiful beaches, which extend almost all the way around its circumference. The most breathtaking ones are on the east coast, stretching along Blockhouse Point, Lizard Point, and Skirt Island. What makes these particular beaches so extraordinary are their colors—the almost white sand, which is made up of tiny shell particles but feels like luxury talcum powder, contrasting with the deep, translucent turquoise of the water. In other parts of the island's perimeter, stray blue agapanthus flowers, escaped from the Abbey Gardens, dot the sand dunes.

This chapter focuses on adding embellishments to your knitting—beads, sequins, and tiny cowry shells like the ones found on the Tresco beaches. The mood we tried to evoke here is one of a summer vacation spent beachcombing on your own Robinson Crusoe island.

> REFRESHMENTS

Abbey Garden Café: Set within the Abbey. Offers snacks and light refreshments. www.tresco.co.uk

Island Hotel: Surrounded by a secluded garden, with its own private beach. The hotel's Terrace Bar, which offers panoramic sea and island views, is open to nonresidents for morning coffee, lunches, and cream teas. www.tresco.co.uk

The New Inn: A centuries-old inn with a pretty subtropical garden. The restaurant specializes in local seafood. The bar serves traditional pub food. www.tresco.co.uk

Tresco stores: Comprehensive selection of food and beverages. Ideal for picnic shopping. www.tresco.co.uk

flippy top

Sizes
S (M, L)

Measurements after Washing
Chest: 33" (35½", 37¾") [84 (90, 96)cm]
Length to top of shaping on front: 18" (19", 19¾") [46 (48, 50)cm]

Materials
- 5 (6, 7) balls Elle True Blue (100% indigo cotton, 1¾ oz [50g], 118 yd [108m]) in Denim
- Size 10 (6mm) needles
- Size 9 (5.5mm) needles
- Size 8 (5mm) needles
- Size 7 (4.5mm) needles
- Size 6 (4mm) needles
- Size 6 (4mm) circular needles
- Miscellaneous beads and sequins for dangles
- Stitch markers

Gauge
20 sts and 28 rows = 4" (10cm) square in st st using size 6 needles before washing.

Abbreviations and Techniques
Refer to pages 18–19.

> This irresistible top fits snugly around the bust, flaring out softly over the waist and hips. It also features adjustable straps at the back, a sexy keyhole front, and a stylish trim that splits into an ornamental bow at the center.

BACK
With size 10 needles, cast on 92 (98, 104) sts.
Beg with a k row, cont in st st.
Work 10 (12, 14) rows.
Change to size 9 needles.
Work 4 rows.
Dec row: K28 (29, 30), skpo, k to last 30 (31, 32) sts, k2tog, k28 (29, 30).
Work 5 rows.
Change to size 8 needles.
Work 4 rows.
Dec row: K28 (29, 30), skpo, k to last 30 (31, 32) sts, k2tog, k28 (29, 30).
Work 9 rows in st st.
Dec row: K28 (29, 30), skpo, k to last 30 (31, 32) sts, k2tog, k28 (29, 30).
Work 1 more row.
Change to size 7 needles.
Work 8 rows.
Dec row: K28 (29, 30), skpo, k to last 30 (31, 32) sts, k2tog, k28 (29, 30).
Work 7 rows.
Change to size 6 needles.
Work 4 (6, 8) rows in st st.**
Inc row: K28 (29, 30), m1, k to last 28 (29, 30) sts, m1, k28 (29, 30).
Work 11 rows even.
Inc row: K28 (29, 30), m1, k to last 28 (29, 30) sts, m1, k28 (29, 30).
Rep the last 12 rows 3 times more—94 (100, 106) sts.
Work 3 rows even.
Bind off.

FRONT
Work as given for Back to **.
Inc row: K28 (29, 30), m1, k to last 28 (29, 30) sts, m1, k28 (29, 30).
Work 11 rows even.
Inc row: K28 (29, 30), m1, k to last 28 (29, 30) sts, m1, k28 (29, 30).
Rep the last 12 rows once more—90 (96, 102) sts.
Work 3 more rows even.

Divide for opening
Next row: K45 (48, 51), turn, work on these sts for left side of Front.
Next row: P to end.
Next row: K to last 2 sts, k2tog.
Work 3 rows even.
Next row: K to last 2 sts, k2tog.
Work 1 row even.
Inc row: K28 (29, 30), m1, k to end.
Work 11 rows even.
Inc row: K28 (29, 30), m1, k to end.
Work 1 row even.
Next row: K to last st, m1, k1.
P1 row.

Shape top
Next row: Bind off 2 sts, k to end.
Next row: Bind off 6 sts, p to end.
Next row: Bind off 2 sts, k to end.
Next row: Bind off 4 sts, p to end.
Rep the last 2 rows once more.
Next row: Bind off 1 st, k to end.
Next row: Bind off 3 sts, p to end.
Next row: Bind off 1 st, k to end.

Next row: Bind off 2 sts, p to end.
Rep the last 2 rows until 3 sts rem.
Next row: Skpo, k1.
P2tog and bind off.
With right side facing, rejoin yarn to rem sts, k to end.
Complete to match first side, reversing shapings.

Edging
With right side facing and size 6 needles, pick up and k28 sts around front opening.
Bind off.

Top/Back Side Edging
Mark 23rd (25th, 27th) st in from each edge of Back.
Starting at point of right front top and with size 6 circular needles, pick up and k19 (21, 23) down "outside" edge of point, 22 (24, 26) sts across Back to marker, cast on 8 sts, then pick up and k48 (50, 52) across Back to marker, cast on 8 sts, pick up and k rem 22 (24, 26) sts across Back, then 19 (21, 23) sts up outside edge of left Front point—146 (152, 158) sts.
Bind off.

LEFT FRONT STRAP
With size 6 needles, cast on 110 (118, 126) sts onto same needle, pick up and k31 (33, 35) sts down left Front top and border, then cast on 45 sts—186 (196, 206) sts.
Bind off.

RIGHT FRONT STRAP
With size 6 needles, cast on 45 sts onto same needle, pick up and k31 (33, 35) sts up border and right Front top, then cast on 110 (118, 126) sts—186 (196, 206) sts.
Bind off.

FINISHING
Join side seams. Thread beads onto a short length of yarn and attach to ties at center Front. Cross long Tie Strap over at Back Strap and tie through loops to fit.

grass bead skirt

Created in wraparound crochet, this skirt includes side ties with crochet strings that have beads and shells attached.

SKIRT

Thread 42 (45, 48) wooden beads onto yarn.

With size F/5 hook, make 130 (139, 148) ch.

Foundation row (WS): Skip 2 ch, 1 sc in each of next 2 ch, *make 14 ch, bring 1 bead up close to hook, skip 1 ch, ss in each of next 13 ch, 1 sc in each of next 3 ch; rep from * to end, turn. Cont in patt.

Row 1: 3 ch, skip 1st dc, 1 dc in each sc to end, 1 dc in 2nd of 2 ch, turn—129 (138, 147) sts.

Row 2: 3 ch, skip 1st dc, 1dc in each dc to end, 1 dc in top of 3 ch, turn.

Row 3: As Row 2.

Row 4: As Row 2, do not turn. Break off yarn.

Thread 42 (45, 48) wooden beads onto yarn.

Row 5: Join yarn to top of 3 ch at beg of 4th row. 2 ch, 1 sc in each of next 2 dc, *make 14 ch, bring one bead up close to hook, skip 1 ch, ss in each of next 13 ch, 1 sc in each of next 3 dc; rep from * to end, turn.

These 5 rows form the patt.

Rows 6–25: Rep Rows 1–5 four times more.

Row 26: As Row 1.

Row 27: 3 ch, 1 dc in each of next 8 (9, 10) dc, [work 2 dc tog, 1 dc in each of next 14 (15, 16) dc] 7 times, work 2 dc tog, 1 dc in each of next 7 (8, 9) dc, 1 dc in top of 3 ch, turn—121 (130, 139) sts.

Rows 28–30: As Row 2.

Row 31: 3 ch, 1 dc in each of next 7 (8, 9) dc, [work 2 dc tog, 1 dc in each of next 13 (14, 15) dc] 7 times, work 2 dc tog, 1 dc in each of next 7 (8, 9) dc, 1 dc in top of 3 ch, turn—113 (122, 131) sts.

Rows 31–33: As Row 2.

Fasten off.

TIES (MAKE 4)

With size F/5 hook and yarn double, make 60 ch.

Leaving long ends, cut off yarn. Thread beads onto long ends and make a knot to secure.

TASSEL

Wind yarn 15 times around the card. Thread length of yarn through needle, then thread through the top end of the Tassel between the yarn and card and tie together to secure Tassel. Cut through bottom end of the Tassel. Wrap the ends from the knot several times around the Tassel and thread the ends through the wrap. Attach to beaded chain.

FINISHING

Join Skirt from hem to Row 26. Attach Tassel to seam to tie.

Sizes
S (M, L)

Measurements after Washing
Waist: 31$\frac{1}{2}$" (33$\frac{1}{2}$", 35$\frac{1}{2}$") [80 (85, 90)cm]
Length: 12" (30cm)

Materials
▸ 6 (6, 7) balls Elle True Blue (100% indigo cotton, 1$\frac{3}{4}$ oz [50g], 118 yd [108m]) in Bone
▸ Size F/5 (4mm) crochet hook
▸ 270 (285, 300) 6mm round wooden beads
▸ Assorted beads and sequins for ties
▸ Piece of card 3$\frac{1}{4}$" (8cm) in diameter

Gauge
16 dc and 8 rows (dc) = 4" (10cm) square in dc using size F/5 hook before washing.

Abbreviations and Techniques
Refer to pages 18–19.

juliet bikini

Sizes
XS–S (S–M, M–L, L–XL)

Measurements after Washing
Bust: 32" (38$\frac{1}{2}$", 45, 51) [81 (98, 114, 130)cm]

Materials
▶ 5 (6, 6, 7) balls Elle True Blue (100% indigo cotton, 1$\frac{1}{2}$ oz [50g], 118 yd [108m]) in Light Denim
▶ Size F/5 (4mm) crochet hook
▶ Assortment of beads and sequins for ties
▶ Piece of card 3$\frac{1}{2}$" (8cm) wide

Gauge
16 dc and 8 rows (dc) = 4" (10cm) square in dc using size F/5 hook before washing.

Abbreviations and Techniques
Refer to pages 18–19.

Strictly for sunbathing, this bikini dispels notions of crochet's sometimes frumpy image. Crochet reflects fashion and indeed *is* fashion. The ties are decorated with shells, sequins, and beads, to resemble beachcombed treasures.

top

LEFT SIDE
With size F/5 hook, make 12 (12, 15, 15) ch.
Foundation row: 1 sc in 2nd ch from hook, 1 sc in each ch to last ch, 3 sc in last ch, working along other side of chain work 1 sc in each ch, turn, 25 (25, 31, 31) sc.
Row 1: Mark center sc on last row. 3 ch, skip 1st sc, 1 dc in each sc to marked sc, 7 dc in marked sc, 1 dc in each sc to end, turn.
Row 2: Mark center dc on last row. 1 ch, 1 sc in each dc to marked dc, 3 sc in marked dc, 1 sc in each dc to end, 1 sc in top of 3 ch, turn.
Rep the last 2 rows 4 (5, 6, 7) times more.
Next row: 1 ch, 1 sc in each of next 2 sc, *3 ch, 1 sc in same place as last sc, 1 sc in each of next 2 sc; rep from * to end, turn.
Next row: Working across row ends, work 30 (36, 42, 48) sc evenly, turn.
Next row: 2 ch, 1 sc in each sc, turn.
Rep the last row twice more.
Fasten off.

RIGHT SIDE
Work as given for Left Side.

TIES (MAKE 5)
With size F/5 hook and yarn double, make 50 ch.
Leaving long ends, cut off yarn.
Thread beads or sequins onto long ends, as desired, and make a knot to secure.

TASSEL
Wind yarn 15 times around a piece of card 3$\frac{1}{2}$" (8cm) wide.
Thread a length of yarn through a needle, thread through the top end of the tassel between the yarn and card, and tie together to secure Tassel. Cut through the bottom end of the Tassel. Wrap the knot ends around Tassel several times, and thread the ends through the wrap.
Attach to beaded chain.
Thread one Tie through loops at front to tie.

FINISHING

Loops (Make 2)
Working into right-hand side of left cup and left-hand side of right cup, attach yarn to end of last row of sc, make 6 ch, ss into end of 1st row, then work 10 sc into loop. Fasten off.
Attach one Tie to each side and each top.

bottom

FRONT

With size F/5 hook, make 10 (11, 12, 13) ch.

Foundation row: 1 dc in 3rd ch from hook, 1 dc in each of next 6 (7, 8, 9) ch, 2 dc in last ch, turn—10 (11, 12, 13) sts.

Row 1: 1 ch, 1 sc in each dc to end, 1 sc in top of 3 ch, turn.

Row 2: 3 ch, skip 1st sc, 1 dc in each sc to end, turn.

Rep the last 2 rows once more.

Row 5: 1 ch, 1 sc in each dc to end, 1 sc in top of 3 ch, turn.

Row 6: 3 ch, 1 dc in 1st sc, 1 dc in each sc to last sc, 2 dc in last sc, turn—12 (13, 14, 15) sts.

Rep the last 2 rows 3 times more—18 (19, 20, 21) sts.

Row 7: As Row 5.

Row 8: 3 ch, skip 1st sc, [2 dc in next sc, 1 dc in each of next 2 sc] twice, 2 dc in next sc, 1 dc in each of next 2 (3, 4, 5) sc, [2 dc in next sc, 1 dc in each of next 2 sc] twice, 2 dc in next sc, 1 dc in last sc, turn—24 (25, 26, 27) sts.

Row 9: As Row 5.

Row 10: 3 ch, skip 1st sc, [2 dc in next sc, 1 dc in each of next 3 sc] twice, 2 dc in next sc, 1 dc in each of next 4 (5, 6, 7) sc, [2 dc in next sc, 1 dc in each of next 3 sc] twice, 2 dc in next sc, 1 dc in last sc, turn—30 (31, 32, 33) sts.

Row 11: As Row 5.

Row 12: 3 ch, skip 1st sc, [2 dc in next sc, 1 dc in each of next 3 sc] 3 times, 2 dc in next sc, 1 dc in each of next 2 (3, 4, 5) sc, [2 dc in next sc, 1 dc in each of next 3 sc] 3 times, 2 dc in next sc, 1 dc in last sc, turn—38 (39, 40, 41) sts.

Row 13: 1 ch, 1 sc in each dc to end, 1 sc in top of 3 ch, turn.

Row 14: 3 ch, 1 dc in 1st sc, 1 dc in each sc to last sc, 2 dc in last sc, turn—40 (41, 42, 43) sts.

Rep the last 2 rows 2 (2, 3, 3) times more.

Next row: 1 ch, 1 sc in each dc to end, 1 sc in top of 3 ch, turn.

Next row: 2 ch, 1 sc in each sc, turn.

Rep the last row twice more.

Fasten off.

BACK

With right side facing, rejoin yarn to 1st, ch, work 1 sc in each ch—8 (9, 10, 11) sts.

Just one of the wonderful beaches on the island of Tresco.

Foundation row: 3 ch, 1 dc in 1st sc, 2 dc in each of next 2 sc, 1 dc in each of next 2 (3, 4, 5) sc, 2 dc in each of next 3 sc, turn—14 (15, 16, 17) sts.

Row 1: 1 ch, 1 sc in each dc to end, 1 sc in top of 3 ch, turn.

Row 2: 3 ch, skip 1st sc, 2 dc in next sc, 1 dc in each of next 3 sc, 2 dc in next sc, 1 dc in each of next 2 (3, 4, 5) sc, 2 dc in next sc, 1 dc in each of next 3 sc, 2 dc in next sc, 1 dc in last sc, turn—18 (19, 20, 21) sts.

Row 3: As Row 1.

Row 4: 3 ch, skip 1st sc, [2 dc in next sc, 1 dc in next sc] 3 times, 2 dc in next sc, 1 dc in each of next 2 (3, 4, 5) sc, [2 dc in next sc, 1 dc in next sc] 3 times, 2 dc in next sc, 1 dc in last sc, turn—26 (27, 28, 29) sts.

Row 5: As Row 1.

Row 6: 3 ch, skip 1st sc, [2 dc in next sc, 1 dc in each of next 2 sc] 3 times, 2 dc in next sc, 1 dc in each of next 4 (5, 6, 7) sc, [2 dc in next sc, 1 dc in each of next 2 sc] 3 times, 2 dc in next sc, 1 dc in last sc, turn—34 (35, 36, 37) sts.

Row 7: As Row 1.

Row 8: 3 ch, 1 dc in 1st sc, 1 dc in each sc to last sc, 2 dc in last sc, turn—36 (37, 38, 39) sts.

Rep the last 2 rows 8 (8, 9, 9) times more.

Next row: 1 ch, 1 sc in each dc to end, 1 sc in top of 3 ch, turn.

Next row: 2 ch, 1 sc in each sc, turn. Rep the last row twice more. Fasten off.

EDGING

Working across row ends, work evenly in sc, turn.

Next row: 1 ch, 1 sc in each of next 2 sc, *3 ch, 1 sc in same place as last sc, 1 sc in each of next sc; rep from * to end, turn.

Fasten off.

FINISHING

Make 4 Ties as given for top. Attach 1 to each side at top edge.

sequined throw

The sequined crochet tassels and the beaded and sequined border are the details that make this throw stand out from the rest. The different colors of weave stitch threaded through the body will prove to be a bit time-consuming. But whether you cozy up with this throw on the beach or on the couch, you'll be glad you made the effort.

Measurements after Washing
Approximately 31½" x 55"
(80x140cm)

Materials
- 9 balls Elle True Blue (100% indigo cotton, 1¾ oz [50g], 118 yd [108m]) in Denim (A), 5 balls in Navy (B), and 6 balls in Light Denim (C)
- Size 5 (3.75mm) needles
- Size 6 (4mm) needles
- Size 7 (4.5mm) needles
- Size F/5 (4mm) crochet hook
- 1,000 size 5/0 glass embroidery beads in white
- 400 8mm cup sequins in silver
- 40 15mm round sequins in silver

Gauge
20 sts and 28 rows = 4" (10cm) square in st st using size 6 needles before washing.

Abbreviations and Techniques
Refer to pages 18–19.

Note
- When adding sequins, bring the sequin up close to the work, knit the stitch, taking the stitch over the yarn and sequin, and letting the sequin hang on the right side of the knitting.
- When placing beads, bring the yarn to the front of the work, then bring the bead up close to the work, slip the next st p-wise, then take the yarn to the back of work.

THROW
With size 5 needles and B, cast on 169 sts.
Moss st row: K1, *p1, k1; rep from * to end.
Rep this row 9 times more.
Change to size 6 needles.
Starting with a k row, work 4 rows in st st.
Thread 200 sequins onto the yarn.
Work Rows 1–9 in st st from Chart A.
Work a further 2 rows in st st.
Cut off B.
Join on C.
Work 4 rows in st st.
Thread 452 beads onto A.
Work 1 row in st st.
Work Rows 1–17 from Chart B.
P 1 row.
Change to size 5 needles.
Starting with a k row, cont in st st and stripes.
Work 24 rows A.
Work 8 rows C.
Change to size 6 needles.
Work 16 rows A.
Change to size 7 needles.
Work 24 rows A.
Work 8 rows C.
Change to size 6 needles.
Work 16 rows B.
Change to size 7 needles.
Work 24 rows A.
Work 8 rows C.
Change to size 6 needles.
Work 16 rows C.

Rep the last 144 rows once more.
Change to size 7 needles.
Work 24 rows A.
Work 8 rows C.
Change to size 6 needles.
Thread 452 beads onto A.
Work 2 rows in st st.
Work Rows 17 to 1 from Chart B.
P 1 row.
Cut off A.
Join on C.
Work 4 rows in st st.
Cut off C.
Join on B.
Work 4 rows in st st.
Work Rows 9 to 1 from Chart A.
Work 1 row in st st.
Change to size 5 needles.
Work 10 rows in moss st.
Bind off.

DANGLES (MAKE 8)
Thread 5 large sequins onto B.
With size F/5 hook, make 12 ch, bring 1st sequin up close to hook, skip 1st ch, ss into each of next 11 ch.
Make 16 ch, bring 2nd sequin up close to hook, skip 1st ch, ss into each of next 15 ch.
Make 20 ch, bring 3rd sequin up close to hook, skip 1st ch, ss into each of next 19 ch.
Make 16 ch, bring 4th sequin up close to hook, skip 1st ch, ss into each of next 15 ch.

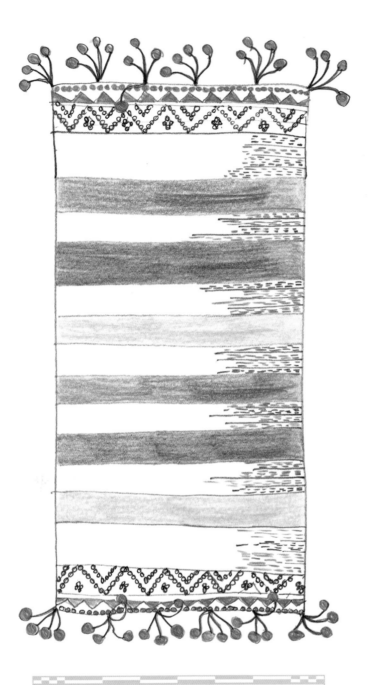

Make 12 ch, bring 5th sequin up close to hook, skip 1st ch, ss into each of next 11 ch.
Fasten off.

FINISHING
Cut 116 lengths each of C and B. Working into each block of 32 rows worked on size 7 needles, taking care not to weave too tightly and weaving under and over every stitch, weave 8 rows of C, 8 rows of B, and 8 rows of C on the 24 rows of A, then weave the 8 rows of C with B.
Attach 1 Dangle to each corner and 4 along each short end.

Chart A

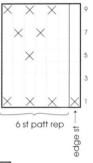

6 st patt rep

edge st

⊠ = place sequin

Chart B

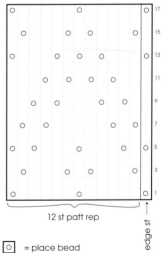

12 st patt rep

edge st

○ = place bead

> **TRESCO GARDENS**

Tresco Abbey Garden: World-class subtropical gardens featuring many plants from the southern hemisphere. Also houses Valhalla, the National Maritime Museum's collection of ship figureheads.
www.tresco.co.uk

sequined cushion cover

This cushion cover is the perfect complement to the Sequined Throw (page 124). It is as wonderful in the living room as it is on the beach.

Measurements after Washing
Approximately 19¾" (50cm) square

Materials
▸ 4 balls Elle True Blue (100% indigo cotton, 1¾ oz [50g], 118 yd [108m]) in Denim (A), 6 balls in Navy (B), and 3 balls in Light Denim (C)
▸ Size 5 (3.75mm) needles
▸ Size 6 (4mm) needles
▸ Size 7 (4½mm) needles
▸ Size F/5 (4mm) crochet hook
▸ 300 small 8mm cup sequins in silver
▸ 20 15mm flat sequins in silver

Gauge
20 sts and 28 rows = 4" (10cm) square in st st using size 6 (4mm) needles before washing.

Abbreviations and Techniques
Refer to pages 18–19.

Note
When adding sequins, bring the sequin up close to the work, knit the stitch, taking the stitch over the yarn and sequin and let the sequin hang on the right side of the knitting.

CUSHION
With size 5 needles and B, cast on 97 sts.
Moss st row: K1, *p1, k1; rep from * to end.
Rep this row 9 times more.
Change to size 6 needles.
Starting with a k row, work 100 rows in st st.
Mark each end of last row with a colored thread.
Change to size 5 needles.
Work 6 rows in moss st.
Change to size 6 needles.
Starting with a k row, work 4 rows in st st.
Thread 145 small sequins onto the yarn.
Work Rows 1–9 from chart in st st.
Work a further 2 rows in st st.
Change to size 7 needles and A.
Starting with a p row, work 108 rows in st st.
Change to size 6 needles and B.
Work 4 rows in st st.
Work Rows 9–1 from chart.
Work 2 rows in st st.
Change to size 5 needles.

Work 6 rows in moss st.
Change to size 6 needles.
Mark each end of last row with a colored thread.
Starting with a k row, work 100 rows in st st.
Change to size 5 needles.
Work 6 rows in moss st. Bind off.

DANGLES (MAKE 4)
Thread 5 large sequins onto B.
With size F/5 hook, make 12 ch, bring 1st sequin up close to hook, skip 1st ch, ss into each of next 11 ch.
Make 16 ch, bring 2nd sequin up close to hook, skip 1st ch, ss into each of next 15 ch.
Make 20 ch, bring 3rd sequin up close to hook, skip 1st ch, ss into each of next 19 ch.
Make 16 ch, bring 4th sequin up close to hook, skip 1st ch, ss into each of next 15ch.
Make 12 ch, bring 5th sequin up close to hook, skip 1st ch, ss into each of next 11 ch.
Bind off.

FINISHING
Cut 54 lengths each of B and C 27½" (70cm) long. Working into the center of the 108 rows worked on size 7 needles, taking care not to weave too tightly and weaving under and over every st, weave [18 rows of C, 18 rows of B] 3 times.
Fold backs of Cushion along marked rows to back of Cushion and join seams.
Attach one Dangle to each corner.

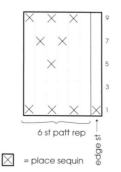

6 st patt rep

edge st

☒ = place sequin

beachcomber flip flops

Covered in the flotsam and jetsam of beach-combed trinkets, these crochet-covered flip flops can be as customized as you like. The pairs shown here include glass, metal, and wooden beads, sequins, and charms.

Materials
▶ 1¾ oz (50g) 118 yd (108m) denim yarn in Ecru or Dark Indigo
▶ Selection of beads and charms
▶ Size F/5 (4mm) crochet hook
▶ Flip-flops

Abbreviations and Techniques
Refer to pages 18–19.

COVERING (MAKE 4)
Make a chain to fit along one side of your flip flop "upper." Work rows of sc until piece will fit around upper comfortably. Bind off.

FINISHING
Sew on selection of beads and charms to cover top of fabric, as shown in photographs.

50°06' NORTH, 5°31' WEST

penzance blue

Penzance, the largest town in West Penwith, Cornwall, lies on the south coast between the villages of Marazion to the east and Newlyn to the west. The town is situated in the middle of Mount's Bay and overlooks the island of St. Michael's Mount.

Penzance is today an attractive seaside town with some very graceful Georgian architecture. Although there is no beach, Penzance has a large harbor and promenade, both of which overlook the enchantingly beautiful island of St. Michael's Mount.

Penzance is also the terminus for ferries and helicopters to the Isles of Scilly and the railway. There are good contemporary art galleries, which are beginning to rival the ones in St. Ives, as well as some excellent stores and restaurants. Historically, Penzance has been a popular resort town. The Jubilee Bathing Pool, built to celebrate the Silver Jubilee of King George V in 1935, is one of the most splendid examples of an art deco lido (an outdoor

Tranquil Prussia Cove, just east of Mount's Bay, Penzance.

swimming pool and sunbathing area made popular in the '30s) still in existence.

When most people think of Penzance, what comes to mind is the Gilbert and Sullivan musical *The Pirates of Penzance*. Indeed, Penzance has a long history of sacking, pillaging, and pirating, mainly by the Spanish, who in 1595 razed the town to the ground. This did not deter the inhabitants of Penzance, however, and what was then a small village grew into a thriving market town, trading by both land and sea. As a result of the regular markets, fairs and festivals sprang up, which continue to this day. In fact, Penzance folk are very fond of having a good time, and at the drop of a hat, will don fancy dress clothes and party! The most famous festival is called Mazey Day, which combines the Feast of St. John with the Summer Solstice and is thus both Christian and pagan. On this holiday, which is held on

RESTAURANTS

The Abbey: Award-winning cuisine combining classical and modern styles. Uses mostly local ingredients. www.theabbeyonline.com

The Bay: Imaginative, award-winning, modern European cuisine. Magnificent views across Mount's Bay. www.bay-penzance.co.uk

The Lime Tree: Modern cuisine inspired by culinary traditions from around the world. Local produce the specialty. www.the-lime-tree.co.uk

the weekend nearest to the Summer Solstice on June 21, candlelit processions wind their way through the town.

Penzance has a special significance for Patrick and me, as it is the place where Patrick's parents lived. It was Freda, Patrick's mother, who was our very first knitting organizer, originally in the village of St. Erth, and later in Penzance. Both Penzance's pirating history as well as the need for sustainable and recycled clothing informed the knits in this chapter. Two of the pieces in the chapter are knit using what we call knitagain yarn, that is, yarn that has been unraveled from an old or unwanted knitted garment, and literally knitted again. Denim yarn, when used as knitagain, has a wonderful quality, as it fades on the outside of the stitch, but retains its strong dyed indigo color from the inside. So, once you unravel the yarn you want to use, you will get what I call a space-dyed effect. If you don't have an old indigo sweater at home already, then look for one on the Internet—eBay is a good source.

Heading west on the South Coast Path.

pirate-stripe guernsey

This two-color striped top features traditional Guernsey detailing around the armholes, a "granddad" button placket, and slit sides. A traditional Guernsey would probably not have an opening at the front, but I think it adds a stylish touch.

Sizes
XS (S, M, L, XL)

Measurements after Washing
Chest: 34½" (37", 40⅛", 45", 41⅛") [88 (94, 102, 112, 124)cm]
Length to shoulder: 24½" (24½", 25¼", 25¼", 26) [62(62, 64, 64, 66)cm]
Sleeve length: 17" (17", 17¼", 17¼", 17¾") [43 (43, 44, 44, 45)cm]

Materials
▸ 7 (7, 8, 9, 10) balls Elle True Blue (100% indigo cotton, 1¾ oz [50g], 118 yd [108m]) in Navy (A) and 6 (6, 7, 8, 9) balls in Denim (B)
▸ Size 5 (3.75mm) needles
▸ Size 6 (4mm) needles
▸ Size 3 (3.25mm) needles
▸ Stitch markers
▸ 5 buttons

Gauge
20 sts and 28 rows = 4" (10cm) square in st st using size 6 needles before washing.

Abbreviations and Techniques
Refer to pages 18–19.

BACK
With size 5 needles and A, cast on 90 (98, 106, 114, 126) sts.
K5 rows.
Join on B.
K6 rows.
With A, k6 rows.
Next row: With B, k8, *p2, k2; rep from * to last 10 sts, p2, k8.
Next row: With B, k6, *p2, k2; rep from * to last 8 sts, p2, k6.
Rep the last 2 rows once more.
Change to size 6 needles.
Cont in st st with garter st borders and stripes of 4 rows A and 4 rows B.
Next row: K to end.
Next row: K6, p to last 6 sts, k6.
Rep the last 2 rows 13 times more.
Cont in st st and stripes of 4 rows A and 4 rows B until Back measures 19¾" (19¾", 20", 20", 20½") [50 (50, 51, 51, 52)cm] from cast-on edge, ending with a p row.

Shape armholes
Bind off 4 sts at beg of next 2 rows—82 (90, 98, 106, 118) sts.
Next row: K2, skpo, k to last 4 sts, k2tog, k2.
Next row: P8, k5, p to last 13 sts, k5, p8.
Next row: K2, skpo, k to last 4 sts, k2tog, k2.
Next row: P7, k5, p to last 12 sts, k5, p7.
Next row: K2, skpo, k to last 4 sts, k2tog, k2.

Next row: P6, k5, p to last 11 sts, k5, p6—76 (84, 92, 100, 112) sts.
Next row: K to end.
Next row: P6, k5, p to last 11 sts, k5, p6.
Rep the last 2 rows until Back measures 28¼" (28¼", 29", 29", 30") [72 (72, 74, 74, 76)cm] from cast-on edge, ending with a wrong-side row.

Shape shoulders
Bind off 16 (19, 22, 25, 30) sts at beg of next 2 rows.
Leave rem 44 (46, 48, 50, 52) sts on a holder.

FRONT
Work as given for Back until Front measures 14½" (14½", 15¼", 15¼", 16") [37 (37, 39, 39, 41)cm] from cast-on edge, ending with a wrong-side row.

Neck opening
Next row: K43 (47, 51, 55, 61), turn, and work on these sts for 1st side of neck opening.
Work even on these sts until Front measures 19¾" (19¾", 20", 20", 20½") [50 (50, 51, 51, 52)cm] from cast-on edge, ending with a p row.

Shape armhole
Bind off 4 sts at beg of next row—39 (43, 47, 51, 57) sts.
Work 1 row.
Next row: K2, skpo, k to end.
Next row: P to last 13 sts, k5, p8.

Next row: K2, skpo, k end.
Next row: P to last 12 sts, k5, p7.
Next row: K2, skpo, k to end.
Next row: P to last 11 sts, k5, p6—36 (40, 44, 48, 54) sts.
Next row: K to end.
Next row: P to last 11 sts, k5, p6.
Rep the last 2 rows until Front measures 23½" (23½", 24½", 24½", 25¼") [60 (60, 62, 62, 64)cm] from cast-on edge, ending with a k row.

Shape neck

Next row: Bind off 10 (11, 12, 13, 14) sts, patt to end.
Keeping garter st band, dec 1 st at neck edge on every row until 16 (19, 22, 25, 30) sts rem.
Work even until Front measures the same as Back to shoulder, ending at armhole edge.
Bind off.
With right side facing, rejoin yarn to rem sts, bind off 4 sts, k to end.
Work even on these sts until Front measures 19¾" (19¾", 20", 20", 20½") [50 (50, 51, 51, 52)cm] from cast-on edge, ending with a k row.

Shape armhole

Bind off 4 sts at beg of next row—39 (43, 47, 51, 57) sts.
Next row: K to last 4 sts, k2tog, k2.
Next row: P8, k5 p to end.
Next row: K to last 4 sts, k2tog, k2.
Next row: P7, k5, p to end.
Next row: K to last 4 sts, k2tog, k2.
Next row: P6, k5, p to end—36 (40, 44, 48, 54) sts.
Next row: K to end.
Next row: P6, k5, p to end.
Rep the last 2 rows until Front measures 23½"(23½", 24½", 24½", 25¼") [60 (60, 62, 62, 64)cm] from cast-on edge, ending with a p row.

Shape neck

Next row: Bind off 10 (11, 12, 13, 14) sts, patt to end.
Dec 1 st at neck edge on every row until 16 (19, 22, 25, 30) sts rem.

Work even until Front measures the same as Back to shoulder, ending at armhole edge.
Bind off.

SLEEVES (MAKE 2)

With size 5 needles and A, cast on 62 (62, 62, 72, 72) sts.
Rib Row 1: K2, *p3, k2; rep from * to end.
Rib Row 2: P2, *k3, p2; rep from * to end.
These 2 rows form the rib.
Work 8 more rows in stripes of 2 rows A, 4 rows B, and 2 rows A.
Next row: With A, k2, *p3, k2, p1, p2 tog, k2; rep from * to end—56 (56, 56, 65, 65) sts.
Next row: With A, *p2, k2, p2, k3; rep from * to last 2 sts, p2.
Work 8 more rows in rib as set in stripes of 4 rows B and 4 rows A.
Next row: With B, k2, *p1, p2 tog, k2, p2, k2; rep from * to end—50 (50, 50, 58, 58) sts.
Next row: With B, p2, *k2, p2, k2, p2; rep from * to end.
Work 6 more rows in rib as set in stripes of 2 rows B and 4 rows A.
Change to size 6 needles.
Beg with a k row, cont in st st and stripes of 4 rows B and 4 rows A.
Work 4 rows.
Inc row: K3, m1, k to last 3 sts, m1, k3.
Work 9 (9, 7, 7, 5) rows.
Rep the last 10 (10, 8, 8, 6) rows until there are 70 (70, 76, 84, 90) sts.
Work even until Sleeve measures 19⅔" (19⅔", 20", 20", 23½") [50 (50, 51, 51, 52)cm] from cast-on edge, ending with a wrong-side row.

Shape Sleeve top

Bind off 4 sts at beg of next 2 rows—62 (62, 68, 76, 82) sts.
Dec 1 st at each end of the next 5 (5, 7, 7, 9) rows then 4 foll alt rows—44 (44, 46, 54, 56) sts.
Dec 1 st at each end of every foll 4th row until 32 (32, 34, 38, 42) sts

rem then on every foll alt row until 28 sts rem.
Dec 1 st at each end of next 3 rows.
Bind off.

FINISHING

Front and neck edging
Join shoulder seams.

Button band
With right side facing, size 3 needles, and B, pick up and k 43 sts down left Front opening.
Row 1: P2, *k2, p2; rep from * to last 5 sts, k2, p3.
Row 2: K3, *p2, k2; rep from * to end.
Break off yarn and leave these sts on a spare needle.

Buttonhole band
With right side facing and size 3 needles and B, pick up and k 43 sts up right Front opening.
Row 1: P3, *k2, p2; rep from * to end.
Row 2: K2, *p2, k2; rep from * to last 5 sts, p2, k3.
Do not break yarn, and leave sts on a spare needle.

Neckband
With right side facing, size 3 needles, and B, pick up and k 3 sts across row ends of buttonhole band, 9 (10, 11, 12, 13) sts from cast-off neck sts, pick up and k26 sts up right Front neck edge, k across 44 (46, 48, 50, 52) sts from Back neck, pick up and k26 sts down left neck edge, 9 (10, 11, 12, 13) sts from cast-off neck sts, 3 sts across row ends of button band—120 (124, 128, 132, 136) sts.
Row 1: P3, *k2, p2; rep from * to last 5 sts, k2, p3.
Row 2: K3, *p2, k2; rep from * to last 5 sts, p2, k3.
Break off yarn, and leave these sts on a holder.

Button band
With right side facing, size 3 needles, and A, pick up and k2 sts across row

ends of neckband, rib across sts of button band.
Work 1 row in rib.
Bind off in rib.

BUTTONHOLE BAND
Mark positions of buttons on button band.
With right side facing, size 3 needles, and A, rib across sts of buttonhole band, pick up and k2 sts across row ends of neckband, *at the same time* make buttonholes to correspond with button placements in this way: *Work to button placement (easiest after p2 sts), keeping yarn at front of work, k next 2 sts tog.
Work 1 row in rib.
Bind off in rib, and do not break off yarn.

Neckband
With right side facing, size 3 needles, and A, pick up and k1 st across row ends of buttonhole band, rib across sts of neckband, pick up and k2 sts across row ends of buttonhole band.
Work 1 row in rib.
Bind off in rib.
Sew on Sleeves. Join side and sleeve seams. Sew on buttons. Loop buttonhole band over button band, and sew in place.

pirate kit bag

This bag has a spiral beaded design, a two-color striped circular base, and drawstring ties. It would make a wonderful beach bag!

Measurements before Washing
Approximately 12" wide x 14" tall (30x35cm), plus Strap

Materials
- 6 balls Elle True Blue (100% indigo cotton, 1¾ oz [50g], 118 yd [108m]) in Navy (A) and 1 ball in Ecru (B)
- Size 5 (3.75mm) circular needles, 32" (80cm) long
- Size 5 (3.75mm) double-pointed needles
- Size E/4 (3.5mm) crochet hook
- 78 glass pony beads (6x4mm) in assorted colors

Gauge
20 sts and 40 rows = 4" (10cm) in garter st (every row k) using size 5 needles before washing.

Abbreviations and Techniques
Refer to pages 18–19.

BASE

With double-pointed needles and B, cast on 8 sts.
Taking care not to twist the yarn, join into a ring.
Mark the join.
Round 1: K into front and back of each st—16sts.
Round 2: P to end.
Join in A.
Round 3: With A, k to end.
Round 4: With A, *pfb, p1; rep from * to end of round—24 sts.
Round 5: With B, k to end.
Round 6: With B, *pfb, p2; rep from * to end of round—32 sts.
Cont in stripes of 2 rounds A and 2 rounds B.
Round 7 and every foll odd round: K to end.
Round 8: P2, *pfb, p3; rep from * to last 2 sts, pfb, p1—40 sts.
Round 10: *Pfb, p4; rep from * to end of round—48 sts.
Round 12: P3, *pfb, p5; rep from * to last 3 sts, pfb, p2—56 sts.
Cont in stripes, increasing 8 sts as set on every p round until there are 248 sts. The increases are staggered to make the base appear as much like concentric circles as possible.
Change to circular needle when necessary.
Break yarn, leaving garter sts on needle.

BODY

Thread beads randomly onto A.
Rejoin yarn to work, but with previous wrong side of work now facing you to prevent beads from falling to purl side (technically the wrong side) of eyelet pattern. When the bag is finished, turn it inside out so both the stripes and the beads are on the right side.
Round 1: *Yo, k2tog; rep from * to end of round.
Round 2: K to end.
Round 3: *[Yo, k2tog] 30 times, push bead up to needle, [yo, k2tog]; rep from * 3 times more.
Round 4: K to end, making sure to knit the yo *before* knitting the bead that lies on it so that the bead lies in the eyelet hole.
The bias the pattern produces will make the beads spiral around the bag.
Rounds 5–6: As Rounds 1 and 2.
These 6 rounds form the patt.
Cont in patt as set until body measures 15¾" (40cm), ending with a k round.
Next round: P to end.
Next round: K to end.
Next round: P to end.
Next round (strap holes): *K6, yo, k2tog; rep from * to end of round.
Next round: P to end.
Next round: K to end.
Next round: P to end.
Bind off k-wise.
Turn bag inside out. Sew in ends securely.

STRAP

With size E/4 hook, make a chain 55" (140cm) long. Work 2 rows single crochet.
Fasten off.
Thread through strap holes on bag, knot together.

sailmaker bolero

We derived the shape for the bolero from an eighteenth-century naval jacket, while the patchwork is inspired by old boat sails that have been patched together to make them seaworthy again. In keeping with the recycling theme, the indigo yarn used comes from an old Artwork sweater, which was unraveled and reknitted. For the overstitching, use a natural-colored linen yarn or even a soft cotton string.

Sizes
S (M, L)

Measurements after washing
Chest: 34" (40⅛", 40") [86, (94, 102)cm]
Length to shoulder: 17" (17¼", 17¾") [43 (44, 45)cm]

Materials
- 5 (5, 6) balls Rowan Denim (100% cotton, 1¾ oz [50g], 108 yd [93m]) in Ecru (A)
- 8¼ (9, 9¾) oz (230 [250, 275]g), 470 (510, 565) yd (430 [465, 515]m)
- Size F/5 (3.75mm) crochet hook
- Waste yarn
- Size 3 (3.25mm) needles
- Size 6 (4mm) needles
- Size 3 (3.25mm) circular needles
- Stitch markers
- 2 large buttons, 1" (2.5cm) in diameter
- 10 small buttons, ⅝" (1.5cm) in diameter
- Sewing needle and thread

Gauge
20 sts and 28 rows = 4" (10cm) square in st st using size 6 needles before washing.

Abbreviations and Techniques
Refer to pages 18–19.

BACK
Using size F/5 hook and A, make 83 (87, 95) ch.
With size 6 needles and waste yarn, pick up a st from each ch except the last one made (as in "crochet cast-on").
Work in patt from chart, and st st, rev st st, and moss st.
Bind off Back neck sts.

FRONTS
With size F/5 hook and waste yarn, make chain 30 (34, 38) ch. Following charts and with size 6 needles, pick up 2 sts for 1st row (as for Back), work 2nd row, and then 1 or 2 sts from the provisional chain according to chart.
Work in patt from chart, keeping side increases correct.

RIGHT SLEEVE

First cuff
With size 3 needles and A, cast on 37 (39, 41) sts.
K4 rows.
Next row: K to last 4 sts, yo, k2tog, k2 to make buttonhole.
K3 rows.
Change to size 6 needles and cont in patt from chart, *at the same time* continuing to work 1st 4 edge sts in garter st for 45 rows, working buttonholes where shown on chart.

Second cuff
With size 3 needles and A, cast on 15 (17, 19) sts.
K8 rows.
Change to size 6 needles and cont from chart, working 1st 4 sts in garter st for button band for 45 rows.
Row 46: Patt 1st 33 (35, 37) sts from 1st cuff, then [work next st tog with first st from 2nd cuff] 4 times, patt to end.
Cont as for chart.

LEFT SLEEVE

First cuff
With size 3 needles and A, cast on 37 (39, 41) sts.
K4 rows.
Next row: K2, yo, k2tog, to make buttonhole, k to end. K3 rows.
Change to size 6 needles and cont in patt from chart, *at the same time* continuing to work 4 edge sts in garter st for 45 rows, working buttonholes where shown on chart.

Second cuff
With size 3 needles and A, cast on 15 (17, 19) sts.
K8 rows.
Change to size 6 needles and cont from chart, working last 4 sts in garter st for button band for 45 rows.
Row 46: Work over 1st 11 (13, 15) sts from 2nd cuff, then [next st tog with

1st st from 2nd cuff] 4 times, patt
to end.
Cont as for chart.

COLLAR AND EDGINGS

Note: This part looks more
complicated than it is. As long as you
mark the correct sts on the Front
hem points and at the beginning of
the V-neck shaping, it won't matter if
you're 1 or 2 sts out in your picking
up. The increases make the hem lie
neatly around the Front points and
the markers at the beginning of the V
help with the main part of the collar
shaping. Keep track as you go of how
many rows you've knitted and you
should sail through it.

Mitered hem

Sew shoulder and side seams.
Beginning at lower left side seam,
with right side facing and size 3
circular needles, remove waste yarn
and pick up and k82 (86, 90) from
provisional cast-on (1 st in each loop)
from back of garment, 29 (33, 37) sts
down right Front hem from provisional cast-on. Mark this last st
(marker 1). Pick up and k48 up right
Front to beginning of Front neck
shaping. Mark this last st (marker 2).
Pick up and k60 (62, 64) up right
Front neck, 4 down right Back neck,
28 (30, 32) across Back neck, 4 up left
Back neck, 60 (62, 64) down left
Front neck, 48 down left Front,
marking the 1st of these 48 sts that
you pick up (to match st marked on
right front, marker 3), 29 (33, 37)
across left Front hem, again marking
the first st picked up (marker 4).
Marked sts should mark the 2 points
on the hem (markers 1 and 4) and the
2 points where neck shaping begins
(markers 2 and 3).
Work back and forth in rows.
Row 1: K to st before marked st, kfb,
k1, kfb, k to st before 4th marked st,
kfb, k1, kfb, k to end.
Row 2: As Row 1.

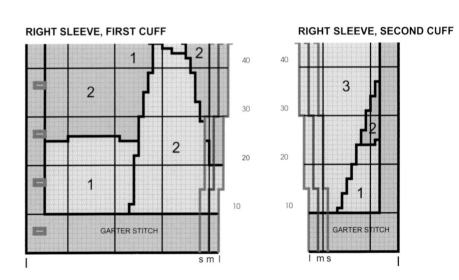

LEFT SLEEVE, FIRST CUFF

LEFT SLEEVE, SECOND CUFF

RIGHT SLEEVE, FIRST CUFF

RIGHT SLEEVE, SECOND CUFF

Row 3: K to end.
Rows 4–6: As Rows 1–3.
Row 7: Bind off sts up to 6 sts before
marker 3 (at the point of the V), k to
next marked st (marker 2), k next 6
sts, bind off rem sts.

COLLAR

Right lapel
Rejoin yarn to rem collar sts on

right-hand side of jacket (right side
of jacket facing, wrong side of collar
facing).
Work back and forth in rows.
Next row: K to end.
Next row: Skpo, k to last 2 sts, k2tog.
Rep the last 2 rows twice more.
Next row: [Skpo] twice, k to last 4 sts
[k2tog] twice.
Next row: K to end.

LEFT AND RIGHT SLEEVE (ROWS 46–184)

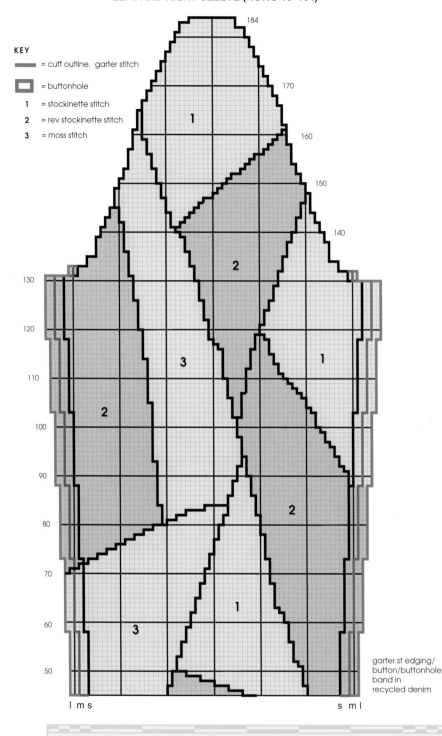

KEY

- ▬ = cuff outline. garter stitch
- ▭ = buttonhole
- 1 = stockinette stitch
- 2 = rev stockinette stitch
- 3 = moss stitch

garter st edging/
button/buttonhole
band in
recycled denim

Right lapel shaping

K41 sts, turn. Work these sts only for
right lapel.

Row 1: K to end.
Row 2: [Skpo] twice, k to end.
Rows 3–4: As Rows 1 and 2.
Row 5: Skpo, k to end.
Row 6: As Row 2.
Row 7: As Row 1.
Rows 8–13: Rep Rows 1 and 2 three
times.
Row 14: Skpo, k to end.
Row 15: K to end.
Rows 16–18: Rep Row 14 three times.
Row 19: K to end.
Row 20: As Row 14.
Rows 21–22: As Rows 19 and 14.
Rows 23–24: K to end.
Rows 25–26: As Row 14.
Rows 27–34: Rep Rows 23–26 twice.
Rows 35–36: K to end.
Rows 37–43: Rep Row 14 seven times.
Row 44: [Skpo] twice, k to last 2 sts,
k2tog.
Row 45: [Skpo] twice, k2tog.
Bind off.

Central collar

Rejoin yarn to rem sts immediately
after the right lapel just knitted, k
across these sts until there are 41 sts
rem on left-hand needle, turn.
Leave these 41 sts for left lapel.
Working on central sts only, k 8 rows.
Bind off.

Left lapel

Rejoin yarn to left lapel, k across
these 41 sts.
Starting at Row 2, work to match
right lapel, reversing shapings.

FINISHING

With B, overstitch the boundaries
between different texture sts on
body and Sleeves. Set in Sleeves, sew
side seams and sleeve seams. Sew
on buttons, sewing lapel buttons on
top of lapels and securing to Fronts
of jacket.

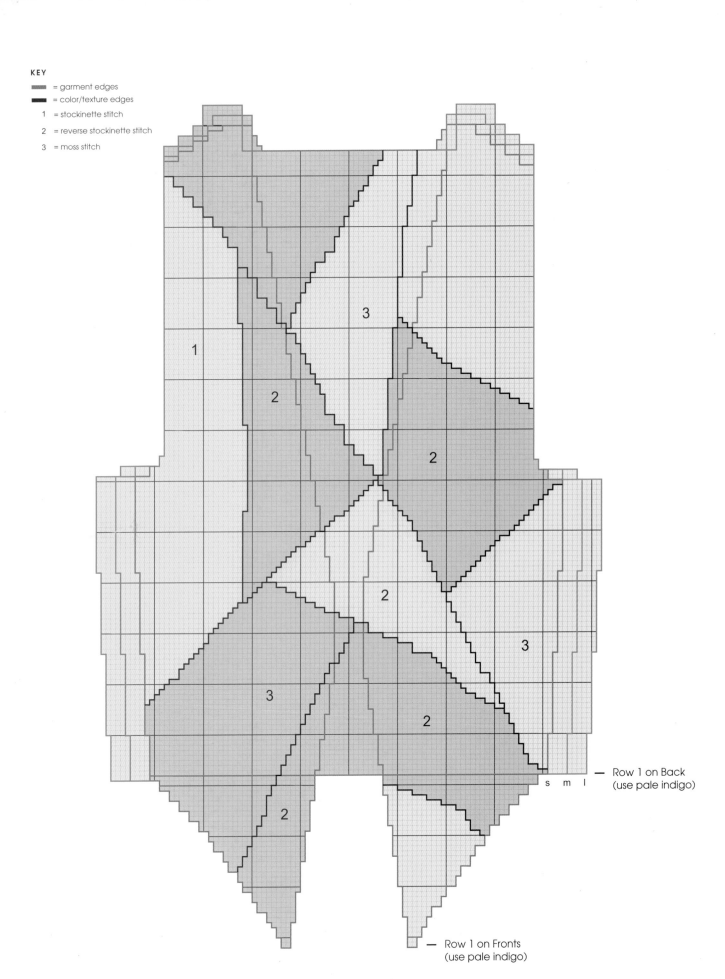

KEY

= garment edges

= color/texture edges

1 = stockinette stitch

2 = reverse stockinette stitch

3 = moss stitch

1

3

2

2

2

2

3

3

2

2

— Row 1 on Back
(use pale indigo)

s m l

— Row 1 on Fronts
(use pale indigo)

grandad cardigan

Long and slim, this comfy cardigan is knitted in a simple design using recycled yarn. The buttons on the front mix the functional with the purely decorative (only every sixth button has a real buttonhole). In our version, we played with different sizes of buttons, but you can also try different shapes and colors—or they can all be the same.

Sizes
XS (S, M, L, XL)

Measurements after Washing
Chest: 34½" (37", 40⅛", 39¼", 41") [86 (94, 102, 112, 124)cm]
Length to shoulder: 24½" (24½", 25¼", 25¼", 26") [62 (62, 63, 63, 66)cm]
Sleeve length: 17" (17", 17¼", 17¼", 17¾") [43 (43, 44, 44, 45)cm]

Materials
▸ 24¾ (26½, 28¼, 30, 31¾) oz (700 [750, 800, 850, 900]g), 1543 (1652, 1761, 1870, 1979) yd (1411 [1511, 1611, 1710, 1810]m) recycled denim yarn
▸ Size 3 (3.25mm) needles
▸ Size 6 (4mm) needles
▸ Size 5 (3.75mm) needles
▸ Stitch holders
▸ Selection of buttons

Gauge
20 sts and 28 rows = 4" (10cm) in st st using size 6 needles before washing.

Abbreviations and Techniques
Refer to pages 18–19.

BACK
With size 3 needles, cast on 88 (94, 102, 112, 124) sts.
K8 rows.
Change to size 6 needles.
Beg with a k row, cont in st st.
Work 140 (140, 142, 142, 144) rows.

Shape armholes
Bind off 3 (3, 4, 4, 5) sts at beg of next 2 rows, 2 sts at beg of foll 2 rows, then 1 st at beg of next 2 (4, 6, 8, 10) rows—76 (80, 84, 92, 100) sts.
Work even for an additional 52 rows.

Shape right shoulder
Next row: K20 (21, 22, 25, 28), turn, and work on these sts for 1st side of neck shaping. Leave rem sts on a holder for Back neck and left shoulder.
Next row: Bind off 1 st, p to end.
Next row: Bind off 9 (9, 10, 12, 13) sts, k to last 2 sts, k2tog.
Next row: P to end.
Next row: Bind off rem 9 (10, 10, 11, 13) sts.
With right side facing, rejoin yarn to rem sts, cast off 36 (38, 40, 42, 44) sts, k to end. Complete to match left shoulder.

POCKET LININGS (MAKE 2)
With size 6 needles, cast on 18 (18, 20, 20, 22) sts.
Work 28 rows in st st.
Leave these sts on a holder.

LEFT FRONT
With size 5 needles, cast on 48 (51, 55, 60, 66) sts.
K8 rows.
Change to size 6 needles.
Next row: K to last 4 sts, slip these sts on a holder for Front band—44 (47, 51, 56, 62) sts.
Beg with a p row, work 29 rows in st st.

Place pocket lining
Next row: K12 (14, 16, 18, 20), slip next 18 (18, 20, 20, 22) sts onto holder for pocket top, k across 18 (18, 20, 20, 22) sts from Pocket Lining, k to end.
Cont even until Front matches Back to armhole shaping (140 rows in st st total).

Shape armhole
Bind off 3 (3, 4, 4, 5) sts at beg of next row, then 2 sts at beg of next right-side row, then 1 st at beg of next 1 (2, 3, 4, 5) right-side rows—38 (40, 42, 46, 50) sts.
Work even for 23 rows with wrong side facing.

Shape neck
Bind off 5 (6, 7, 8, 9) sts at beg of next row, then 3 sts on foll 2 wrong-side rows, then 2 sts 3 times, then 1 st 3 times—18 (19, 20, 23, 26) sts.
Work until Front matches Back to shoulder, ending at armhole edge.

prussian naval jacket

This jacket was inspired by an eighteenth-century naval jacket, though the original would not have been knitted or beaded, of course. The beading technique used here is particularly helpful when the beads are too large to lie flat across the stitch—it gives the beads a better finish than just sewing would.

Sizes
S (M, L)

Measurements after Washing
Chest: 31½" (34", 36¼") [80 (86, 92)cm]
Length to shoulder: 19" (19¾", 20½") [48 (50, 52)cm]
Sleeve length: 17" (17¼", 17¾") [43 (44, 45)cm]

Materials
12 (13, 14) balls Elle True Blue (100% indigo cotton, 1¾ oz [50g], 118 yd [108m]) in Navy
Size 3 (3.25mm) needles
Size 6 (4mm) needles
Size 5 (3.75mm) needles
Size E/4 (3.5mm) crochet hook
Stitch holders
Sewing needle and thread
300 beads

Gauge
22 sts and 32 rows = 4" (10cm) square in st st using size 6 needles before washing.

Abbreviations and Techniques
Refer to pages 18–19.

BACK

With size 3 needles, cast on 89 (95, 101) sts.
Moss st row: K1, *p1, k1; rep from * to end.
Rep this row 5 times more.
Change to size 6 needles.
Beg with a k row, cont in st st.
Work 4 (6, 8) rows.
Dec row: K2, skpo, k to last 2 sts, k2tog, k2.
Work 9 rows.
Rep the last 10 rows once more and the dec row again.
Work 13 (15, 17) rows.
Next row: K2, *m1, k to last 2 sts, m1, k2.
Work 9 rows.
Rep the last 10 rows once more and the inc row again.
Work a further 7 rows.

Shape armholes
Bind off 1 st at beg of next 8 (10, 12) rows—81 (85, 89) sts.
Work 76 rows even.

Shape shoulders
Bind off 4 sts at beg of next 8 rows.
Next row: Bind off 4, knit next 4 (5, 6) sts, turn and work on these sts for 1st side of Back neck—5 (6, 7) sts.
Next row: Bind off 1, p to end.
Bind off rem 4 (5, 6) sts.
With right side facing, rejoin yarn to rem sts, bind off center 31 (33, 35) sts, k to end.

Next row: Cast off 4 sts, p to end.
Next row: Cast off 1 st, p to end.
Bind off rem 4 (5, 6) sts.

LEFT FRONT

With size 3 needles, cast on 33 (36, 39) sts.
Moss st row 1: K1 (0, 1), *p1, k1; rep from * to end.
Moss st row 2: *K1, p1; rep from * to last 1 (0, 1) sts, k1 (0, 1).
Rep the last 2 rows twice more.
Change to size 6 needles.
Next row: K29 (32, 35), leave rem 4 sts on a safety pin for front band.

Front shaping
Next row: P2, w&t.
Next row: K1, kfb—3 sts active.
Next row: P5, w&t.
Next row: K5.
Next row: P7, w&t.
Next row: K7.
Next row: P9, w&t.
Next row: K8, kfb—10 sts active.
Next row: P12, w&t.
Next row: K12.
Next row: P14, w&t.
Next row: K14.
Next row: P16, w&t.
Next row: K16.
Next row: P18, w&t.
Next row: K17, kfb—19 sts active.
Cont this way, working 2 sts more on each p row until 25 (27, 29) sts are worked before the w&t.

Back

Next row: K24 (26, 28), kfb.
Next row: P28 (30, 32), w&t.
Next row: K28 (30, 32).
Next row: P to end. Place marker at the end of this row.
Cont in st st, increasing 1 st at center Front edge on foll 5th row and then every foll 10th row after that until there are 39 (42, 45) sts.
Work even until 62 (66, 70) rows have been worked from marker.

Shape armhole
Bind off 1 st at beg of next and 3 (4, 5) foll alt rows—35 (37, 39) sts.
Work even 60 rows, ending wrong side facing for next row.

Shape neck
Next row: Bind off 4 (5, 6) sts, p to end.
Next row: K to end.
Next row: Bind off 3 sts, p to end.
Next row: K to end.
Next row: Bind off 1 st, p to end.
Next row: K to end.
Rep the last 2 rows 3 times more—24 (25, 26) sts.
Work 5 rows.

Shape shoulder
Bind off 4 sts at beg of next and 4 foll alt rows.
Work 1 row.
Bind off rem 4 (5, 6) sts.

RIGHT FRONT
With size 3 needles, cast on 33 (36, 39) sts.
Moss st Row 1: K1 (0, 1), *p1, k1; rep from * to end.
Moss st Row 2: *K1, p1; rep from * to last 1 (0, 1) sts, k1 (0, 1).
Rep the last 2 rows twice more.
Change to size 6 needles.

Front shaping
Next row: K2, w&t.
Next row: Pfb, p1—3 sts active.
Next row: K5, w&t.
Next row: P5.
Next row: K7, w&t.
Next row: P7.

Complete to match left Front, reversing all shapings.

LEFT FRONT BORDER

With right side facing and size 3 needles, slip sts from safety pin onto a needle, inc in 1st st, patt rem 3 sts—5 sts.
Cont in moss st until band fits neatly up to beg of neck shapings when slightly stretched, ending with a wrong-side row and sewing neatly into place as you go.
Leave sts on holder for collar.

RIGHT FRONT BORDER

With wrong side facing and with size 3 needles, slip sts from safety pin onto a needle, inc in first st, patt rem 3 sts—5 sts.
Cont in moss st until band fits neatly up to beg of neck shapings when slightly stretched, ending with a wrong-side row and sewing neatly into place as you go.
Leave sts on holder for collar. Do not break off yarn.

COLLAR

Join shoulder seams.
With right side facing and size 3 needles, patt across 3 sts from right Front band, work next 2 sts tog, then pick up and k21 sts up right Front neck, 3 sts down right Back neck, 31 (33, 35) sts across Back neck, 3 sts from left Back neck, 21 sts down left Front neck, work 1st two sts on left Front band holder tog, patt across rem 3 sts—87 (89, 91) sts.
Work 10 rows moss st, dec 1 st at each end of every foll alt row.
Next row (WS): K to mark hemline. K next row to make a fold line.
Work 10 rows moss st, dec 1 st at each end of every foll alt row.
Bind off loosely in patt.

SLEEVES (MAKE 2)

With size 3 needles, cast on 48 (52, 56) sts.

Moss st row: K1, *p1, k1; rep from * to end.
Rep this row 3 times more.
Change to size 5 needles.
Work 8 rows moss st.
Change to size 6 needles.
Beg with a k row, cont in st st.
Work 4 rows.
Change to size 5 needles.
Work 12 rows in moss st.
Change to size 6 needles.
Beg with a k row, cont in st st.
Work 4 rows.
Next row: K2, m1, k to last 2 sts, m1, k2.
Work 3 rows even.
Rep the last 4 rows 17 (18, 19) times more and the inc row again—66 (72, 78) sts. Work 5 rows even.

Shape Sleeve top
Bind off 3 sts at beg of next 2 rows, and 2 sts on foll 4 rows—52 (58, 64) sts.
Next row: K2, k2tog, k to last 4 sts, skpo, k2.
Next row: P to end.
Next row: K2, k2tog, k to last 4 sts, skpo, k2.
Work 3 rows even.
Rep these 4 rows 8 (9, 10) times more—32 (36, 40) sts.

Next row: K2, k2tog, k to last 4 sts, skpo, k2.
Next row: P to end.
Rep the last 2 rows 3 times more—24 (28, 32) sts.
Bind off 2 sts at beg of next 6 (8, 10) rows.
Bind off rem 12 sts.

FINISHING

Set in Sleeves. Sew side and sleeve seams.

TRIMS

Thread beads onto yarn, and with size E/4 hook, make 1 chain, push bead right up to hook, make chain around bead. Rep until bead chain is long enough to fit around cuff, fasten off. Make 3 more bands.
Sew bead chain into st st band on cuff.
Sew another bead chain to 2nd row of st st above moss st border.
Make another bead chain long enough to fit all around edge of jacket, as shown in photograph, and sew on. Make another bead chain for front swirl, sew into place, make another to match.
Fold collar in half to wrong side and slip st carefully into place.

acknowledgments

Patrick, my partner in every way, for his stunning photography that captures the essence of modern Cornwall.

Penny Hill and Belinda Boaden, our extraordinarily clever pattern writers, who remained calm and patient throughout!

Our sample knitters, Ivy Fletcher, Frances Jago, and Audrey Yates, for their amazing skills. They have been with us through thick and thin for approximately twenty years. We also need to mention Audrey's fabulous embroidery.

Jules York Moore, for hair and make-up.

Anna, Clare, Dexter, Guy, Hannah, Johnny, Kate, Lorna, and Tom, our wonderful bunch of models, who we pulled off the beaches, dragged out of bars, and spotted in cafés!

Holly Young, who assisted on the Newlyn and Lamorna photo shoots.

Annika Shaw and Stella Maris, for their help and general encouragement.

The Tresco Estate Office, which provided us with all we needed for our day shooting the Tresco chapter, including the great golf cart for getting around on!

The "Bag of Rags" pirate boat we used as a location in the Penzance chapter.

Robert Jones, for letting us use one of his paintings from the Penwith Gallery, St. Ives.

Kathleen, for letting us use the Penwith Gallery as a location for the St. Ives chapter.

The Old Mill at Lamorna, for use of their beautiful garden as a location in the Lamorna chapter.

Louise Watkiss from Kitts Couture (www.kittscouture.co.uk), for loan of some of her gorgeous vintage clothes.

Tom and Will, our two sons, for putting up with very fractious and non-resident parents!

Christina Schoen, our wonderful editor, who guided us through the making of this book.

Joy Tutela, our fantastic agent, who has guided two novices through the literary world, which is so different from that of fashion!

resources

The following guide, compiled by our friends at Potter Craft, will help you locate the yarns needed to complete the projects in the book.

FOR ROWAN DENIM AND ROWAN HANDKNIT COTTON DK:
Rowan yarns are readily available at fine yarn stores across the country. Visit www.knitrowan.com for a complete list of stockists in the United States, the UK, and around the globe!

FOR DEN-M-NIT BY ELANN:
Den-M-Nit is available at the Elann website (www.elann.com). Please note, however, Elann is known for their excellent pricing so supplies sell out quickly. Refer to the yarn substitution guide below in the event that Den-M-Nit is unavailable.

FOR TRUE BLUE BY ELLE:
Elle yarns are distributed by Unicorn Books and Crafts (www.unicornbooks.com). To place an order in the United States, call 800-289-9276. If you're in the UK, visit www.knit1now.co.uk or call 00 44 (0)1376 573802.

yarn substitutions

All the indigo-dyed yarns called for in this book can be used interchangeably. Brands such as Marks & Kattens Indigo Jeans DK and GarnStudio Den-M-Nit also work well as substitutes. If you'd like to experiment with other yarn substitutions, whether indigo-dyed or not, try 100 percent unmercerized cotton yarn with a matching gauge *and* similar shrinkage properties. Remember: All the yarns called for in this book are DK-weight or light-worsted-weight and shrink 20 percent after washing. Since the amount of yarn per skein varies, be sure to base your substitution on the total yardage called for rather than the number of skeins.

To determine whether a yarn with shrinking properties is a suitable substitute, make a large swatch. Then, using a loose running stitch and thread in a contrasting color, mark off a square measuring at least 4" by 4" (10cmx10cm). Then wash and dry the swatch as you would a finished garment (instructions on page 12). To calculate the shrinkage, subtract the original length of the swatch from the new length of the swatch and divide that number by the original length. Multiply by 100 to get the shinkage percent.

project index

This guide, organized by chapter, offers you a quick glimpse of the projects in the book.

index